WOMEN *of* DESIGN

WOMEN *of* DESIGN

CONTEMPORARY AMERICAN INTERIORS

Beverly Russell

Foreword by Andrée Putman

RIZZOLI
NEW YORK

For the next generation:
Angi Bates, Jasmine Redfern

First published in the United States of America in 1992 by
Rizzoli International Publications, Inc.
300 Park Avenue South, New York, NY 10010

Library of Congress Cataloging-in-Publication Data

Russell, Beverly.
Women of design : contemporary American interiors /
Beverly Russell ; foreword by Andrée Putman.
p. cm.
Includes bibliographical references and index.
ISBN 0-8478-1614-1
1. Women interior decorators—United States. 2. Interior
decoration—United States—History—20th century—Themes,
motives. I. Title.
IN PROCESS
729'.082—dc20   92-8177
CIP

Frontispiece: Kitchen, San Francisco residence,
designed by Lucia Howard/Ace Architects.
Photograph by Alan Weintraub.

Designed by Betty Lew

Printed in Singapore

I wish to thank Lois Brown of Rizzoli International Publications, New York, for encouraging me to take on this subject. I have been delighted to work with editor Robert Janjigian and graphic designer Betty Lew on this project. Both have enthusiastically contributed to its form and content.

I applaud the many women who have been very helpful to me while putting together this book: Dominique Lalli, my researcher, who spent long hours in libraries making sure that I read every relevant publication about women and design; Emily Pearl, an excellent copy editor, who contributed thoughtful criticism; Gretchen Bellinger, who went so far as to arrange a two-day retreat at her camp in the Adirondacks at which a small group discussed the book's potential content; Margaret McCurry, for her stern criticism on drafts of the introduction; Patricia Conway, who was always there, despite numerous commitments, ready to comment in writing on various aspects of the text as it developed; Amla Sanghvi, for her picture research; Andrée Putman, who received me graciously in Paris for an interview that resulted in the book's foreword; Susana Torre, who evaluated my ideas with her academic eye; Alexia Lalli, for her unfailing support; and Barbara Tober, my first employer in the United States, who has been an inspiring mentor since 1967.

As an independent working mother since the 1960s, I readily identify with the struggles of the women profiled, and I salute their efforts and achievements. Their stories have given me strength to continue along the path, "having perhaps the better claim, because it was grassy and wanted wear . . . ."

Foreword 8

Introduction 9

ECLECTICS

Leslie Armstrong *16, 32*

Josephine Carmen & Clara Igonda *18, 36*

Karen Daroff *20, 40*

Margo Grant *22, 44*

Kitty Hawks *24, 48*

Debra Lehman-Smith *26, 52*

Dian Love *28, 56*

Eva Maddox *30, 60*

PURISTS

Martha Burns *64, 80*

Lee Foster-Crowder *66, 84*

Dorothy Harris *68, 88*

Spes Mekus *70, 92*

Julia Monk *72, 96*

Rita St. Clair *74, 100*

Lynn Wilson *76, 104*

Trisha Wilson *78, 108*

MINIMALISTS

Clodagh *112, 128*

Carol Groh *114, 132*

Margaret Helfand *116, 136*

Carolyn Iu *118, 140*

Stephanie Mallis *120, 144*

Elizabeth McClintock *122, 148*

Sylvia Owen *124, 152*

Lella Vignelli *126, 156*

POETS

Pamela Babey *160, 176*

Gretchen Bellinger *162, 182*

Patricia Conway *164, 188*

Frances Halsband *166, 194*

Lucia Howard *168, 198*

Naomi Leff *170, 204*

Phyllis Martin-Vegue *172, 210*

Margaret McCurry *174, 214*

Directory 218

Bibliography 220

Index 221

My own search for an independent identity began at a very young age. I was eleven when I began to question the style and taste of my parents' house, with its big drawing room filled with antiques. I thought to myself, "Are there rules that oblige me to behave like this, to marry in my group and live in this locality, in this way?" I quickly made up my mind that this nostalgia was not for me. I went often to visit the house of one of my school friends, whose father was an intellectual. They lived in a Robert Mallet-Stevens-designed apartment, filled with amazing furnishings and objects. The place had an air of peace, charm, and serenity that I didn't find in my parents' house or the houses of their friends. So that was the beginning of my approach to a style.

If you choose to belong to the environment of your family and your background, life is easy, no nasty remarks are made about you, and you are in harmony with your group. But you don't have that inner strength that you get from being apart. When you are apart you are a target, so you learn to build up strength.

I found myself apart from the time I was a young girl. It has always been my nature to want to change the world, to cross barriers, to reconcile periods of history, to bring people together who would never meet for all kinds of reasons, people who belonged in separate worlds. I have learned that being on the outside does not mean being stupid, lost, or angry, or hurt or bitter. With this life comes freedom. So people either take me as I am or they don't take me at all. Therefore, I never had to prove that I was as good as a man. There was no struggle for me because I have never felt weak in front of men. I have never felt intimidated or a victim of social harassment. I think that to practice interior design successfully as a woman is a matter of psychology. I am so passionate about what I propose and so involved and too emotional about a project. My convictions are too intense to leave any place to worry about how I am going to deal with men. That never comes to my mind.

I made a Freudian slip when I named my own firm *Ecart*, meaning "marginal" or "on the side"—in other words, I put myself out of the mainstream. As soon as I set up my business in 1979 I was credible, even though I only had one employee. People immediately understood my position, my belief in being modern, and I was suddenly accepted, although before nobody believed me at all. The wave that took me up was very powerful. I never believed I was great, but I was sure my ideas were great, and I was so strongly convinced that I took on a crusade for these great ideas—the designs of Mallet-Stevens, Eileen Grey, Pierre Chareau, and others. I was fortunate, because in the eighties, people were hungry for new people, new ideas, and new images.

I have continued to hold on to my identity, and I am almost religious in the way I approach my work. The process is not purely intuitive, nor is it intellectual. There is an energy in it, but there is also the spirit of the crusade. I have never made concessions on a job or accepted a job just for money, because I could not wake up in the morning and see that I had done something poor, without poetry and charm.

Although, as we look back on this century, it is evident that there have been decades of struggle for women to achieve identity, it is also clear that the feminist movement has not worked. I have never belonged to women's liberation or taken part in street demonstrations, because I always believed it was too aggressive and only made things worse—like putting oil on a fire. I prefer the more French approach, which is to fight for yourself. When you get hurt, you get a recipe for how not to be hurt twice. By taking the aggressive approach, women have lost the chance to enjoy life—because it is difficult to enjoy life if you are heartless. But worse, the possibility of wonderful relationships with men, that special, sensitive relationship of friendship that we call in France *copine*, has also been lost. Perhaps it would be better to put less attention on gender. My life has always been looking for art and new ideas in other people's work, whether male or female. I have made many people famous, and I didn't expect any recognition. Perhaps my story is in the category of a fairy tale, but it has been amazingly rewarding.

Andrée Putman
Paris, January 1992

Into the Ninth Decade

It is a almost a century since the first woman in the United States took up interior design as a serious, money-earning proposition. Today, interior design is at the center of intellectual debate for acceptance as a legitimate discipline alongside architecture, which has a history dating back thousands of years. We've come a long way . . . since Elsie de Wolfe, an actress and a social butterfly in her twenties and thirties, with a reputation as a woman of style, taste, and imagination, kicked off her own decorating firm at the age of almost forty in 1907.

From selecting antiques in Paris and London for rich New York City patrons, such as the Fricks, Astors, and Vanderbilts, de Wolfe branched out into interior design, beginning with the exclusive women's Colony Club on Park Avenue. At first, the members of the club were startled and dismayed by her approach. At a time of heavy Victorian tasseled draperies, dark furniture, Turkish boudoirs, and ornamental exaggeration, her light pastel-shaded rooms presented a totally fresh image. They contained a minimum of wall hangings and were filled with English garden-theme chintzes, sometimes innovatively

Elsie de Wolfe. Photograph courtesy of the Museum of the City of New York, The Theater Collection.

Edith Wharton. Photograph courtesy of The New York Public Library.

Julia Morgan. Photograph courtesy of Special Collections, California Polytechnic State University.

used as slipcovers, and trellised walls resembling Italian gardens or French orangeries. It was all quite radical. But de Wolfe persisted with her ideas, requesting that the club members not change things around until the rooms were completely finished. When the club was done, it quickly became the talk of the town. And its success enabled Elsie de Wolfe to put out her shingle. Indeed, her business card, depicting a wolf with a flower in its jaw, became legendary on both sides of the Atlantic until her death in 1950.

De Wolfe was not the only woman to show an interest in interior design at the turn of the century. The novelist Edith Wharton collaborated with architect Ogden Codman, Jr., on *The Decoration of Houses*, a practical handbook, in 1902. It was a book that spoke to the revolution of the time. "No study of house-decoration as a branch of architecture has for at least fifty years been published in England or America," the authors pointed out. They emphasized the "notable development in

Denise Scott Brown.

Beverly Willis. Photograph by Russell Fischella.

architecture and decoration" that had been going on in the past ten years. They deplored the division of labor that led to the architect being responsible for the interior elevations, floor plans, and detailing, with the upholsterer being called in to decorate and furnish the rooms. But they applauded the advent of professional decorators who understood the fundamental principles of their art. Their book went on to tell readers how to resolve the decoration and design of walls, doors, windows, fireplaces, ceilings, floors, entrances, vestibules, halls, stairs, drawing rooms, gala rooms, libraries, dining rooms, bedrooms, and even schoolrooms and nurseries. Copious historical illustrations of rooms and furniture, allied with masterly prose, combined to make this book the interior design bible of its time.

There was no question that Elsie de Wolfe was much influenced by Wharton and Codman when writing her own book, *The House in Good Taste*, published in 1913. Later, in her autobiography, *After All*, published in 1935, she recalled that when asked to bring her first book up to date she replied, "There is nothing to change but the picture. My creed is the same today as it was. The principles of beauty do not change. Form, space, proportion, light, air, prospect, purpose, these are values with which they are concerned. And they remain the same, whether they are applied to the composition of a poem or a song, of a painting or a cathedral."

Gender Divisions

As the century rolled along, women took a strong lead in residential interior design, and through their imaginations, they helped establish America's worldwide reputation in this decorative art. It can be argued that men furthered their success, finding interior design an acceptable occupation for women by reason of its connection to domesticity, at a time when women were asserting their independence in the working world. By the end of the nineteenth century, the traditional work of the home had undergone dramatic changes. Factories produced many of the goods women had once made themselves, school attendance had become compulsory, professions were established, and social services were created. The home became an arena for the woman with more ambitious desires than to be a house-

wife and mother. With more sophisticated means of running the home (washing machines and other newfangled devices) at her disposal, and less domestic staff to help out, the "housewife" could legitimately raise her status to that of "home efficiency expert." And the supervision of the interior design of the house was a responsibility included in this agenda.

While many women did not call for gender "liberation," the handful who led the crusade to develop the new domestic management scenario saw the prospect as a starting point for progressive social improvement on many levels. As a result of this serious recognition for the newly established occupation, however, an insidious schism developed that was to align architecture with the masculine gender and interior design with the feminine gender for the rest of the century. To be sure, women inched into architecture, notably Louisa Bethune (1856–1913), Catherine Beecher (1800–78), and Julia Morgan (1872–1957) of San Francisco, who designed more than 700 buildings in her lifetime, including William Randolph Hearst's famous castle at San Simeon, but it was a long hard road to recognition and acceptance, as prominent contemporary women architects, such as Denise Scott Brown, Beverly Willis, and others will confirm. In her 1989 essay, "Room at the Top," Scott Brown, thirty years into her career, commented: "For me . . . discrimination continues at about the rate of one incident a day." Willis, the only practicing woman architect in San Francisco from the sixties to mid-seventies, noted that in 1991, "women are still playing catch-up to the big-firm institutionalization of architecture created by men." Men's attitudes about turf and territory affected many of the women portrayed in this book. As architecture students in the 1960s, some were the targets of chauvinistic attacks by professors who tried to direct them out of schools of architecture and into interior design departments, under the pretext that they were never likely to practice and thus were taking away places in class from men who were more deserving.

While many women persevered and passed their architecture exams, few went on to become practicing architects, as the current statistics of the American Institute of Architects (AIA) confirm. Today, women constitute 9.1 percent of all AIA members—5,003, out of a total of 55,036 (according to 1991 records)—and this figure, small as it is, represents a twelvefold increase since 1970! The fact that women and men are now represented in equal numbers in some architecture schools indicates that the tide has turned, but even so, it is noteworthy that few of these women continue on into the profession. Evidently, many find it too difficult to move forward in their careers in male-dominated architecture firms. The majority of women working in such firms are not partners or associates responsible for design, according to an editorial in the October 1991 issue of *Architecture* magazine. Denied opportunity, and wishing to maintain their integrity and self-confidence, many start their own businesses.

Most of the women profiled in this book studied architecture but then went on to run their own firms, specializing in interiors. As the decades have passed, the work that these highly qualified women have undertaken has developed dramatically. Women of design are no longer predominantly "ladies with hats," cavorting in Café Society, having tea with wealthy patrons. Nor, with the rising affluence of the middle classes, are they making their living as just "corner store" decorators. They most definitely do not *only* "do houses"— although this is not to say that decorators who concentrate in this area are not doing perfectly valid work. The essays in this book were written to demonstrate that interior design has branched out and moved far beyond the era of Elsie de Wolfe and her gilded boudoir-bathrooms—"moonshine and glamour, white orchids and rock crystal, silver tissues and white furs, reflected in many mirrors!"

A New Direction

It was the equally legendary Florence Schust Knoll who steered the design profession along a different path. Born in

Florence Knoll. Photograph courtesy of The Knoll Group.

Michigan and trained at the Cranbrook Academy, where she befriended Finnish architects Eliel and Eero Saarinen, she went on to London to study architecture at the Architectural Association. Driven back to the United States during her third year of study by the outbreak of World War II, she completed her degree under Ludwig Mies van der Rohe at the Illinois Institute of Technology in Chicago. She met her future husband, Hans Knoll, who had established a furniture company in 1939 in New York under his name, while working with the distinguished New York architecture firm of Harrison & Abramowitz.

In 1943 she became a partner in the Knoll Company and established the Knoll Planning Unit to handle its interior design operations. It was the beginning of a whole new business: commercial interior design. Knoll crusaded for contemporary modern design—furniture and textiles that fitted into the International Style glass-skin buildings that became emblematic of post-World War II corporate America. She attracted architects and designers of international importance to design furniture for the firm. During the fifties and sixties Knoll expanded to twenty showrooms in the United States and thirty abroad, and the Knoll Planning Unit specialized in working with architects to fit out interiors. It was the start of what was to become a $40-billion-a-year-plus industry by the 1980s, and the beginning of a tremendous opportunity for women to establish themselves in a legitimate profession.

As commercial interior design firms were established in the 1960s, separate from architecture firms and geared to offer special services for corporate and commercial clients in virtu-

ally every field, from the hotel industry to the hospital and health-care professions, to manufacturing and retail, it was a new cadre of women who staffed them. Male architects considered the work an inferior pursuit, with its feminine associations of coziness and domesticity. Women graduates from both architecture and interior design schools filled the gap. And they learned, for the most part, on the job. No school had trained them for the new work that they were undertaking. It was a far cry from choosing paint chips and textiles, hanging up a chandelier, deciding where to place a mirror, or fitting out a clothes closet. As for the history of interior decoration, while the principles that Elsie de Wolfe cited as unchanging still applied, the 1960s' fashion for Modernism hardly allowed for experiments in historicism. (That was yet to come, in the ritzy Postmodernist era of the 1980s.)

Commercial design acquired its own body of knowledge, which was refined over the next thirty years. As architects became more esoteric, commercial interior designers delved into ductwork, telecommunications, mechanical and electrical systems, construction documents, computer-assisted design, ergonomics, food and beverage service, and other back-of-the-house facilities, such as restaurant kitchens and commercial laundries. In short, they were in charge of all services into the building and out into the street. Given the bare shell of a structure, with hundreds or sometimes thousands of users to accommodate, they were responsible for laying out floors, selecting the best locations for all the services and departments, and perhaps most important of all, enhancing the quality of life, health, and safety of the people who were ultimately to use the space.

They also had to keep up with the mind-boggling expansion of the furniture industry. By the late 1970s the world of office furniture systems had grown from the lines offered by the design leaders Knoll and Herman Miller to more than 150 options, with each firm insisting that it had the best to offer. New legislation passed in the eighties forced interior designers to become familiar with energy-conscious products and with life-safety innovations in order to protect their clients from potential lawsuits by users or employees. The Americans with Disabilities Act, passed in Congress in early 1992, made it mandatory for all public places to be universally accessible. Resource libraries containing a vast array of information, as well as actual samples of fabrics, laminates, lighting, carpeting, marbles, and other materials, became integral elements in commercial design firms, bringing a new dimension into specifying, which had previously been done by architects, who referred to a volume of catalogs known as *Sweet's*.

Economic Indicators

In the recessions of 1974 and 1981, the same architects who had despised the world of interiors when there were opportunities to swagger with black cape à la Frank Lloyd Wright and captivate millionaire patrons/developers, or to build America for the federal government, turned to remodeling, which almost

Ruth Lynford. Photograph by William Whitehurst.

always included interior renovation and design. It was a way to keep afloat in an uncertain, idiosyncratic business. But in 1990, when the next economic dip occurred, they were shocked to find themselves in competition with some very astute professional interior designers—who were mostly women.

In fact, the writing had been on the wall for at least six years, since 1984, when legislation was first enacted in the state of Alabama recognizing interior design as a legitimate profession. As the legislation gathered momentum in other states, architects who had ignored it at the beginning began to sense the strength of the crusade and line up vociferously against it, citing architects as the only people with sufficient knowledge and education to practice interior design. Battles were fought—and won—by the interior designers, who proceeded to establish similar legislation in sixteen states by 1992.

None was as tough in terms of passage as the bill in New York State, guided for more than six years by a determined woman architect and interior designer, Ruth Lynford. New York, with a large number of interior designers (10,000), was seen as a bellwether state and thus one in which architects should take a stand. That Ruth Lynford pitted herself and her small coalition of six interior design organizations against the mighty AIA and emerged successful is a lesson in the power of persistence, tactics, and sheer charisma on her part. "I was taught to take risks, to put your life on the line for what you feel is right. I just had to do what I had to do," she explains. Once New York, Illinois, and California were in the bag in 1990, there was no turning back. Interior design was on the docket as a full-fledged profession, subject to specific exams and government regulation. It was no longer enough to be a woman of style and taste, to practice as, and call oneself, an interior designer.

Of course, architects argued and continue to voice the opinion that interior design education is inadequate and in no way matches the depth and breadth of the architectural curriculum. And many interior designers, and architects practicing interior design, agree with them, despite the fact that there are now well over ninety schools in the country accredited by the Foundation for Interior Design Education Research (FIDER), which monitors degree programs on a constant basis. The two-, three-, and four-year programs are no match for the intellectually layered postgraduate degrees in architecture, however. It must be remembered, though, that architects, during their extensive schooling, learn very little about interior design. It is often offered as an elective, frequently overlooked and generally considered, as previously noted, "unmasculine." If it were otherwise, the interiors of so many institutional and public spaces that we all inhabit—in schools, libraries, hospitals, railway stations, and airports, for example—would be more sympathetic and sensitive to mood and atmosphere. As one example, take hospitals. While it has been proved in Europe that subtle use of color can actually help patients get well, for the most part the people in charge of American hospital design continue to pursue prison typologies. Generally, therefore, the argument that architects, by dint of their long, arduous education, are the only people who can come to grips with interior design, is a self-perpetuating myth.

Recognition for Women

The women's movement in this century has gone through various incarnations, which is as it should be in an evolving, dynamic world. From the early "one-person-one-vote" days, there has been constant reevaluation of what an independent, self-fulfilled woman is and what it is she wants in life. In Elaine Showalter's *These Modern Women*, a collection of autobiographical essays from the mid-1920s by women who were seeking self-definition (many through professional writing, as it was the easiest and most acceptable way of combining home, family, and career in those days), it is frequently suggested that the providing of day care is the responsibility of the employer. The time lag on the implementation of that idea was sixty years! Only in the mid-1980s, through the activism of women lawyers on behalf of their colleagues, was the provision of day care established as a reasonable and expected procedure in the business world. By then, it was hard to hold out, since women comprised more than 40 percent of the work force and were essential in keeping the United States moving in its postindustrial, service-oriented track.

Similarly, the reluctance to concede that women deserve recognition in the world of design, as individuals who bring sense and authority to the subject, seems to be slowly vanishing. Things generally change when fresh economic factors emerge. The news, reported in a 1988 AIA report, *Vision 2000*, that most of the buildings for the year 2000 were already up, suddenly turned the focus toward remodeling and interiors as the source of architectural revenue for the future. The fact that only about 9 percent of the organization's members were women was an economic indicator to the AIA that women must be solicited if the organization was to continue to gain strength. (It was noted that 72 percent of the members of the 33,000-strong American Society of Interior Designers [ASID] were women, many of whom had some architectural training.)

Put these two statistics together and one can begin to understand why a profession-

Susan Maxman.

al revolution is currently in progress, one that will affect the practice of both architecture and interior design. In 1992 the AIA elected the first woman national president in its 134-year history—Susan Maxman. At the local chapter level, there were twenty-seven women presidents, compared to eleven in 1985, and twenty new Women in Architecture committees were formed. In the same year, four prestigious academic strongholds of architecture and design surrendered to females: the deanships at the University of Pennsylvania (Patricia Conway), the Pratt Institute (Frances Halsband), the University of California at San Diego (Adele Santos), and the Parsons School of Design (Susana Torre).

The sudden appearance of prominent mid-career women in academia heralds a new understanding of the social, political, and economic forces that are coming together to shift the male hegemony in the profession. For women in architecture (many of whom, like the women in this book, are working in the interior design field), this shift is a clarion call to a new order: the reconnection of a long-stigmatized profession with architecture, from which, intellectually, it never should have been separated. And for Susana Torre, who was denied tenure at Columbia University's School of Architecture, her appointment at Parsons is a vindication of her outstanding contribution to academia. These new deans for the nineties will certainly bring refreshing attitudes to the educational process, promising to shift the focus away from the individual "star" system and toward a more collaborative, problem-solving mode. They seek to transform the nature of pedagogy, and with it the way architects approach and think about the built environment. "And maybe," says Torre, "there will come a time when we no longer have separate and different voices, but a richness of discourse that is not exclusionary."

Susan Maxman's opportunity to boost the female membership in the AIA, and thus grant recognition to a more diverse profession, signals a new respect for women architects who practice interior design—many of whom have been too intimidated to join the organization, which has been a male bastion for so many years. "Too much emphasis has been placed on the star system," claims Maxman. "We must make the public understand that architects do much more than design beautiful façades. I'd love to see this organization become a place for all who make architecture happen. It must include not only architects in private practice but developers, educators, facility managers, and others who shape the environment."

The Narrative Idea

To explore the new role of women academicians and their effect on the future of design education, textile designer Gretchen Bellinger hosted a two-day retreat during the summer of 1991 at her "camp" in the Adirondack Mountains, to which Patricia Conway and Susana Torre were invited, along with two other women profiled in this book, Pamela Babey and Phyllis Martin-Vegue, from San Francisco. Both deans expressed their belief that the discipline of interior design would gain strength in the next decade. "It is a much richer field than architecture," Conway pointed out. "You turn over a space in five to ten years, whereas a building is up for decades. There are so many more opportunities to refine ideas." Pamela Babey noted that male architects who joined her interior design firm, Babey Moulton, were always amazed at what the discipline offered. "They finally understand, once they work with us, that furniture ordering and furniture plans are the last ten minutes of the job. It's a revelation."

Susana Torre confirmed that under her direction, the established Western canon of architectural discourse taught at Parsons School of Design is now being expanded to contain other points of view. "And by exploring narratives, you can look at interior design in a serious way, so that it does not become devalued in the architectural program," she explains. "Opportunities to explore the narrative, to tell a story, produce a finer grain of interior design."

This connection with story telling is perhaps one reason why interior design has become a female domain over the years. In some of the recent dialogues about gender differences, it has been postulated that from infancy to adolescence, boys and girls demonstrate very different attitudes and engage in very different activities, particularly where communication is concerned. Girls like to tell stories and exchange secrets with their best friends. Boys tend to express themselves more directly. They like to be involved in sports and to compete with one another. From an early age, femininity is defined as "self-in-relationship," with the result that women tend to view themselves as care-givers, who must respond to the needs of others and make sure that no one gets hurt. Conversely, masculinity is defined as differentiation and separation from the mother, which in turn leads to separation from the "other" and the world. Boys are more concerned that everyone be treated fairly—hence the male ethic of justice, as opposed to the female ethic of caring.

The latest studies, in fact, throw a monkey wrench in the works for those who stand resolutely by the belief that the sexes can and should be equal. For it appears that they never can be. Studies of male and female brains reveal anatomical differences that have correlates in emotional responses. Men apparently don't have the same neurological ability to record the most sensitive emotional experiences. According to Dr. Deborah Tannen, professor of linguistics and author of the book *You Just Don't Understand: Women and Men in Conversation*, the sexes have different "but equally valid styles."

While the goal of equality may still be the crusade, the diehards must recognize the differences between the sexes—and exploit them—before more ground can be won. Yet only recently, studies in leadership by the International Women's Forum (published in the *Harvard Business Review*) noting the difference between male and female leadership techniques, were contested by some women, who argued against the facts! "Pretending that women and men are the same hurts women because the ways they are treated are based on the norms for

Sarah Tomerlin Lee.

Diane Legge. Photograph by
Stuart-Rodgers-Reilly.

Jane Graham.

Jane Thompson. Photograph by Jon Goell.

men. It also hurts men who, with good intentions, speak to women as they would to men," declares Dr. Tannen. "Recognizing gender differences frees individuals from the burden of individual pathology. Only by understanding each other's styles and our own options can we begin to realize our opportunities."

Future Consolidation

After a century of evolution, interior design is poised on the brink of a revolution, paralleling the women's movement, facing the issues of sexual harassment, pro-choice, and macho power plays in which men circle the wagons to protect their hegemony when encountering female assertiveness. Central to the success of the profession will be the much-discussed unification of all those involved in the design process at any level—as Le Corbusier expressed it, "everything from the city to a teaspoon." The value of design itself is constantly undermined by the lack of support for individual disciplines within the design world. The person out on the street, asked to define what an architect does, or to name a leader in the profession, will probably be hard-pressed to come up with a reply. Yet shelter is one of three primary human needs! There is obviously a major communications gap in need of some bridging.

It has been proven that minority rights are gained when minorities support one another. There is strength in numbers. Unfortunately, counterproductive, bickering factions and inter-professional wars are not uncommon in the history of design. At the beginning of the century there were two design organizations, one for men and one for women. In 1931 the American Institute of Decorators, which included both sexes, was formed. In 1958, after twenty-five years in existence, when the Institute's executive committee refused to abide by the members' wishes to change its appellation to the American Institute of Interior Designers, a rival organization, the National Society of Interiors Designers, was established. It was not until 1975 that the two organizations saw the wisdom of joining together to form one great American Society of Interior Designers (ASID). Today a variety of special interest groups exists in the profession, including the Institute of Business Designers, the

International Society of Interior Designers, and the Institute of Store Planners. A target date of 1995 has been set for unification, which will bring political strength and increased public recognition to the umbrella organization. Meanwhile, the Interiors Committee of the AIA continues to expand its chapters, and many of these chapters organize annual awards programs to focus on the value of interior architecture.

In Closeup

While the women in this book present a coherent picture of the strength of the profession, their biographies indicate the broad spectrum of education and experience typical of the discipline's evolution. Their degrees may be in architecture, environmental planning, urban planning, liberal arts, interior design, fine arts, or the school of hands-on building. Only three of the thirty-three are employed by a large firm. The remaining thirty operate their own companies, with employees varying in number from six to one-hundred-thirty-six. They are all in mid-career, with from fifteen to twenty-five years of hard work behind them. It would be foolish to imagine that they are the only distinguished women in practice, however. The narrow focus of the book, with its parameters of mid-career, award-winning, American women working mainly in the field of commercial interior design, limited the number of portraits to be included. Significant women who are not portrayed should be mentioned: Sister Parish, founder of Parish-Hadley; Betty Sherrill, president of McMillen; Sarah Tomerlin Lee, president of Tom Lee; Diane Legge Kemp, who in 1982 was the first woman to be named partner at Skidmore Owings & Merrill; Jane Graham, who ran the interiors department of Skidmore Owings & Merrill's Chicago office in the 1950s; Kirsten Childs, a recent trailblazer in ecologically sound design; and Jane Thompson, who helped her architect partner, Benjamin Thompson, in the creation of the shopping-as-entertainment malls developed in Boston, Baltimore, New York, and elsewhere by the Rouse Company; are just a few of the many women who have made a significant mark in the evolution of the profession.

To identify their work with more clarity, the thirty-three professionals profiled have been arranged in four sections: Poets, Eclectics, Purists, and Minimalists.

Poets are generally unpredictable and seem not to follow any established rules of design. Rather, they prefer to make up their own rules on a project-by-project basis. They stretch their imaginations in several directions and are particularly sensitive to qualities of color and craftsmanship. They share a passion for detail and innovation. Poets work on distinctive projects that call for a designer who will not bring a predictable approach to the job: unusual corporate offices, retail operations, educational installations, museums, galleries, and libraries.

Eclectics are versatile designers who are happy to cross disciplines, moving from architecture, to product and graphic design, and even to fine art and architecture. They like to experiment with different materials and forms and are not afraid to make strong statements. Their spaces are not just backgrounds but attempts to match the personalities of their clients. Eclectics generally come from diverse backgrounds and bring a broad perspective to the job. They are ingenious problem solvers, always seeking to find new ways to respond to a client's situation. They can handle a range of projects, from corporate installations to showrooms to hotels.

Purists adhere to more traditional notions of beauty and comfort. They know how to work in historical styles and are well versed in antique furnishings and classical detailing. They also respect the historicist attitudes of more recent times, the Postmodernist bent for ornamentation, decoration, and color. In this category are designers who work in the hotel and restaurant field, the entertainment and leisure industries, and the high-end corporate area. They know how to manipulate different levels of luxury, fantasy, and excitement to capture the public's interest.

Minimalists are most comfortable working out their ideas in pared-down Modern style, with a minimum of ornament, decoration, and color. They are experts in the art of making design with high-energy impact. Their work provides a neutral background against which people provide the color. These designers are much sought after by clients who want a vocabulary that presents an image of "forwardness," of being "on the leading edge." This approach can be applied to various types of interiors—from corporate office projects and banking facilities to restaurants, showrooms, and retail stores.

When I set out to write this book, and identified the group of thirty-three women to be profiled, reactions from the

"Women of Design" at Camp Bellinger, Long Lake, New York, (left to right): Patricia Conway, Susana Torre, Phyllis Martin-Vegue, Gretchen Bellinger, and Pamela Babey.

design community were varied. Mostly there was amazement that there actually were so many women who qualified for inclusion in the book, by reason of their stature and influence. One sentiment that many of these women expressed in the interviewing process was disappointment that they had received little support from other women. Many had encountered jealousy, sabotage, unfriendliness, and other negative emotions and experiences. Pamela Babey admitted candidly, "I've encountered more loyalty from men than I have from women in my career. Back-stabbing can come from the very women you have tried to help in developing their careers!"

In 1991 the historic Judge Clarence Thomas vote in the Senate, and the public reaction to the discrediting of Professor Anita Hill (both men *and* women voted against her in the polls) pointed up the ambivalence that many women still have toward working women who are out there competing with men. As Jennifer Barker Woolger and Dr. Roger J. Woolger put it in their study *The Goddess Within:* "The majority of women, whether they work or not, feel most fulfilled in their primary roles as wives, partners, and mothers." In the same year, however, Hollywood produced the Ridley Scott–directed film *Thelma and Louise*, a movie that captured a *Time* magazine cover story and generated debate in universities and research institutes across the country. Its central characters were two gutsy women who decided that there was no going back to diapers and dishes, to wife abuse and subordination—that literally "going over the cliff" was a more dignified alternative. By so doing, they articulated a new phase in the feminist movement, because they were seen as representative of typical, everyday women, not feminist intellectuals. Their militancy certainly caught on with legions of "ordinary" women, in whom the heroic actions of these nonheroic women struck a chord. The Woolgers speak in their book of the "compelling inner pressures" that both sexes are now under to understand their gender differences. They add: "These forces are being felt powerfully by women and in a different way by men, transforming the most fundamental ways we think about ourselves."

While we have come a long way, we certainly still have a long way to go. I wrote this book as a salute to all those Women of Design who have taken the risks—as an inspiration for all those who will choose the same independent route tomorrow.

Leslie **Armstrong**

Taste comes in many flavors for Eclectics. These

versatile designers are usually accomplished in

multiple design disciplines. They are

experimenters—with new materials, forms, and

concepts of space—and are not afraid to make

strong statements. They create interactive

environments in which space is not necessarily

enlivened solely by its user. Eclectics attempt

to capture the client's personality in

three dimensions.

L eslie Armstrong's interests have been strongly influenced by the evolution of the women's movement. As the decades of the 1970s and 1980s rolled along, she found she was better able to express her belief in the value of interior design, which the male-dominated profession of architecture frowned on as being beneath its dignity. "At first I conceded reluctantly that my best work was involved in the shaping, articulation, and fleshing out of interior space, but now it is with a mix of relief and pride that I acknowledge interior design as my forte," she explains. "Women are managers, and they think micro, while men think macro. Females care about how somebody's home works for them. Most architects think micro aspects of a residential project will take care of themselves, but they're wrong. For example, I can't imagine doing a house without laying out all the closets, belt by belt, shoe rack by shoe rack, even in a tiny little apartment." It is this attention to detail that helped win Armstrong the job of supervising architect on a recently completed $7-million two-house complex in Fairfield, Connecticut, for Rolling Stone Keith Richards and his partner, Patti Hanson. Armstrong's responsibilities included doing shop drawings for all the cabinetwork, planning the mega-kitchen/family room, administration of the project team, and budget control of the project, which was shielded from media exposure to ensure the rock star's privacy.

Growing up with a father who was a doctor and a mother who was (and still is) a practicing lawyer, Armstrong decided at age ten that, since she didn't want to be like either of her parents, she would be an architect. But what she loved most was the "inside" of architecture. An understanding of just what that could include was brought home to her as a teenager aboard the liner *Andrea Doria* in 1953, crossing the Atlantic on a journey to Italy. She was entranced by the tile work around the pool, the mill work in the cabins, the table settings and glassware in the dining rooms. This was her introduction to modern Italian design—"design that synthesizes past and present, function and aesthetics, interior and exterior space," as she puts it.

After earning a bachelor's degree with honors in fine arts from Brown University and briefly flirting with a career in the theater and performing arts, Armstrong enrolled at Columbia University's School of Architecture, graduating in 1972. The interlude with the world of drama, in particular her interaction with stage management and set building, has informed her design work ever since. She applies color confidently on every job, creating unusual backgrounds that have become her special signature. Her own office is approached through an elevator lobby and entrance foyer painted in deep green with trim in yellow and peach tones, a scheme that is repeated in the laminate tops used for the reception area and the conference rooms.

Above: Executive dining room in the Henry Holt & Company publishing offices, New York City. Photograph by Norman McGrath.

mauve. Her plan, which rotated a box within a box, articulated by an overhead grid of yellow and green to express the program further, produced four functional zones: private work space with appropriate shelving and file storage, formal and informal conference areas, secretarial support space, and dressing and vanity-service closet. The environment had a perceptibly feminine aura, yet the format was such that it could easily serve the opposite sex. Armstrong had shown how a woman's creative ideas and thinking could enhance the working environment for *both* sexes—if men were willing to go beyond corporate stereotypes to respond to an innovative, original work space.

Armstrong has always practiced in small New York City firms with no more than a dozen people on staff. She has weathered three economic recessions (1974, 1981, 1991) and is still going strong, pursuing clients, working out her passions, and frequently getting published, not only as the subject of articles about her work but as the author of two books—*The Little House* (Macmillan, 1979) and *Space for Dance* (Publishing Center for Cultural Resources, 1984). Since 1985 she has served on the board of trustees of Robert College in Istanbul, founded by American educator Cyrus Hamilton in 1863 as a prep school. Her responsibilities have included steering the board through five new-building projects, and she is currently supervising renovation of five older ones.

A turning point in Armstrong's career, specifically in her ability to feel truly comfortable in the interior design arena, came in 1984, when she was selected by *Interiors* magazine to create a prototypical office for the executive woman. She had already proved herself to be more than competent at remodeling and creating residential interior spaces and was beginning to inch her way into the realm of corporate office design, with a 33,000-square-foot space for the publishing company Henry Holt, in which she demonstrated how color (peach and three shades of gray) could wrap through an interior and provide continuity on a low budget. The *Interiors* project was cosponsored by *Working Woman*, a mass-circulation magazine that wanted to reinforce the rising status of women at the corporate level. At that moment in history, hot debate was in progress as to whether a woman's professional environment should respond to more feminine ideas of leadership and work style, or whether it should emulate the corporate man's scenario for success (and thus categorize executive women forever as "clones"). Accepting the *pro bono* invitation with her customary crusading enthusiasm, Armstrong held out strongly for a feminine identity for the space. It was a moment for self-evaluation—for analyzing where she, herself, was going.

Armstrong's design didn't offer "peach prettiness" but went for a more gutsy, complex palette. Resolutely avoiding a monochromatic, typically male, color scheme, she chose silver and dark gray, augmented with yellow, fir green, purple, and

Armstrong's penchant for the "micro" is suited to the demands of performing arts (a specialty developed over the past twenty years), where details such as the depth and composition of the floor, and the organization of back and front stages, catwalks, riggings, and aprons, are crucial for ensuring optimal performing conditions. A project for the Wilmington Grand Opera, which won her an AIA award, was notable for its faithful renovation, even down to re-creating the original decorative frescoes, which were reinterpreted from written descriptions, painted on canvas, and applied like wallpaper. But if her solicitous eye can be trained on everything, down to the comfort of an auditorium chair, there is another side to Armstrong that characterizes other aspects of her work. After collaborating for nine months in the mid-1970s with the renowned architect Alan Buchsbaum, she caught his spirit for often-bizarre juxtapositions of materials and furnishings. Buchsbaum liked to innovate, introducing kitsch furniture, industrial objects, and found pieces into his spaces. His ideas gave Armstrong the courage "to make funny moments within tranquility."

Armstrong likes to develop ideas from a surrounding context and then push them to a radically different place—"to sing an aria rather than deliver a speech in prose," she says. Some examples: a coffee table might have a corner cutaway because the room is narrow and needs more circulation space; a nursery carpet cutaway reveals linoleum, to create designated play space. For her own weekend house in Massachusetts, a fireplace mantel in several shades of plastic laminate takes the form of swagged curtains. It is "very rich, because it's simple and complicated at the same time," she notes, "like a Beethoven quartet"—though she admits that it took her some hours and her best sales technique to convince her doctor-husband to accept this eccentricity. She typifies the woman architect working in a small firm with a diverse practice, who is forever striving to reinvent the parameters of design.

A selection of Armstrong's work appears on pages 32 to 35.

MILA PENN

Josephine **Carmen**
Clara **Igonda**

Above: Conference room, Leastec Inc. offices, Los Angeles, California. Photograph by Paul Bielenberg.

On the Hollywood Walk of Fame, in the center of California's film capital, where the celebrities' names appear on plaques in the sidewalk, there is still a strong sense of the magic of yesteryear—the golden age of the movies during the 1930s. And in a building on the corner of North Cherokee, art deco ziggurat motifs and colors are etched in the lobby and the elevators, totally unchanged since the period. Emerging from the elevator into the third-floor corridor, the sense of bygone days is even stronger—you feel as if you've somehow wandered into a Raymond Chandler film. A row of oak-framed opaque glass doors, with original hardware, recalls the classic private-eye office. Josephine Carmen and Clara Igonda, whose design firm is located here, wisely decided not to eliminate the doors but to capitalize on them, so that clients could enjoy the building's architectural history. The unconventional approach suits their image. They are, perhaps, an unlikely combination in Los Angeles: Carmen, a designer from London, England, and Igonda, an architect from San Juan, Argentina, partnered with John Farnum, a California industrial designer who directs the business side of the firm. However, they exude an international vitality and also have impressive credentials. They met at Walker Associates, a Los Angeles firm, in the 1980s, after both had worked in half a dozen other American firms.

"In 1988 we felt it was time to start our own office, but [we wanted] to keep it small, so that as principals we could control the boards, very much as designers and not figure-heads," says Carmen. "We never want to be more than sixteen to twenty people. We believe this personal touch is what clients are looking for today." In the short period of their existence, the firm has zoomed forward, winning an Institute of Business Designers (IBD) award for the design of the Stendig furniture showroom at the Pacific Design Center in 1990. Recently completed and current projects include three restaurants, a fitness club, and a hotel in Japan, the retail complex Niketown in Chicago, law offices for Paul, Hastings, Janofsky & Walker in Los Angeles, new headquarters for Act III Communications, a 40,000-square-foot job in Century City, several showrooms, and an eye clinic. It's a varied portfolio of corporate, retail, hospitality, institutional, showroom, and health-care facilities—and Carmen and Igonda intend to keep it that way. They also offer a variety of services—color selection, art consulting, product design, and graphics. Both having trained abroad, in countries where design education emphasizes a "holistic" approach, rather than a compartmentalized attitude to separate disciplines, they are prepared to respond to multiple requests.

In the highly competitive atmosphere of the design industry in Los Angeles, presentation is, of course, everything. In response to this, Carmen and Igonda developed a handsome logo that is used consistently to establish their image: a gray square with the firm's name embossed on it. The same format is employed in the neat six-inch square folders that contain promotional materials, as well as in the box kits used to sell the firm's work. The partners never show slides of their work, as they are convinced that clients will not remember who did what, if they have asked several firms to interview. And the trick to getting a job, they believe, is to be remembered. When receiving visitors at their own offices, or when invited to see a client, they produce two handsome fifteen-inch square boxes, reiterating the gray color and the square graphic of their firm's logo. Each box contains high-quality dry-mounted color photographs of five recently completed jobs. "We walk through the work, maintaining eye contact the whole time with the client," says Carmen. "We feel it's much more effective than projecting slides with dimmed lighting. The tactile dimension, the act of handing the boards around the table, is also helpful, we think, to a successful presentation and more convincing for getting the commission."

Asked to describe their work and influences, Carmen identifies Louis Beal, formerly a partner at ISD in the 1960s and 1970s, as a very important mentor during her thirty-year career. "I worked for ISD in New York when they launched out as the first true commercial design firm, breaking away from decorative arts. Louis Beal was one of the early people who had a vision of how interior design could become refined." Igonda cites the late Paul Kenyon of CRSS, where she worked for two years in the 1970s, as having had an astonishing effect on her thinking: "I was his assistant, and at that point moved from architecture into interiors because Paul felt it was better for me. I had studied architecture in order to change the world. But Paul helped me focus on the way the space could be done, with a total relationship to architecture—the materials, furniture, art, and lighting—and I found it was very satisfying."

Carmen and Igonda would never deliver a "traditional" interior, but that is not to say they are capable of offering only a Modern vocabulary. They say they are "grounded in Modern style," but that is just the bare bones of what they are about. "We haven't got a mission statement yet, because we feel we should respond to individual situations," says Igonda. "If we sense a client wants something a bit more decorative, of course we will do it, in our own way. For instance, we just did a job with sponge technique on the walls and a cut-limestone floor—the traditional qualities in a fresh way. But on the whole we take our cues from what already exists in the architecture of the job. We will not go out of our way to be different, just for the sake of being different."

One area they relish getting into is health care, which they feel is ready for major rethinking. They point to the new "expertise" of way-finding, which is now used to make hospitals less intimidating, but which they believe is just a cosmetic approach to covering a fundamental failing in the design of a hospital building. "If designers were doing their jobs properly, and architects were laying out the buildings properly, patterns to destinations would be evident, through lighting, landscaping, color, and forms. People would not have to read multiple signs, which is an enormous challenge, to find their way around," Carmen reasons. She subscribes to health-care design that takes its signals from the ancient monasteries, which were

Above: Stairway detail, Sitmar Cruises offices, Los Angeles, California. Photograph by Jon Miller, Hedrich-Blessing.

the original hospitals, resonating with peacefulness and a healing atmosphere. "We want to capture that kind of pleasant atmosphere of wide corridors, views from windows, mellow lighting, and color. Monasteries are simple—plaster walls, stone floors, quiet colors—but so easy to keep clean that there is no reason why the ideas shouldn't be copied today."

As a minority business, fifty-one percent owned by women, Carmen and Igonda's firm is well positioned for the kind of substantial hospital work they have in mind. "It gives us an additional edge when big jobs come up for joint ventures with architects who are most likely to get the architectural commissions for state and county public buildings," says Carmen. "Women in business are now beginning to get into the action."

A selection of Carmen and Igonda's work appears on pages 36 to 39.

SEYMOUR MEDNICK

Karen **Daroff**

Above: The Levy Gallery, Moore College of Art & Design, Philadelphia, Pennsylvania. Photograph by Jon Naar.

aking her acceptance speech for *Interiors* magazine's Designer of the Year award, before an audience of 1,000 designers and architects at the Waldorf-Astoria Hotel in New York City on February 1, 1990, Karen Daroff commented not on aesthetics but on investments. She emphasized that the profession of interior design had evolved into a formidable and complex business, where the accouterments of electronic systems such as CAD and marketing savvy were no longer options or luxuries, but essentials.

Daroff's outspoken remarks represented a turning point for the 1990s. The design profession had matured. It was no longer an esoteric art, practiced exclusively by creative people in a vacuum. Successful firms such as Philadelphia's Daroff Design Inc., which has been in business since 1973, have learned to meet clients on *their* level. They market themselves as corporations market. They budget as corporations budget. They use the most sophisticated automated systems available. They have CEOs, CFOs, public relations consultants, marketing experts, and the entire raft of support staff required to manage a business efficiently and profitably. "Profitability," said Daroff, "is the result of excellence on all levels. And you cannot stay in business unless you make a profit."

Daroff didn't always have this strong bottom-line attitude. Like most people who choose a career in design, she had no business training whatsoever (an astonishing fact, given that statistics indicate the most talented college graduates will go into business on their own after an average of seven years spent working for other firms), and she initially made no efforts to increase her business acumen, relying on "design excellence" to ensure her firm's survival in the marketplace. Since the 1980s, however, she has been on the leading edge of the trend toward "designer-as-businessperson," a role model for her peers.

Fresh out of Philadelphia's Moore College of Art in 1968, Daroff took a job with Vincent Kling, now retired chairman of the Kling-Lindquist Partnership, who became her mentor. The firm worked on major architectural jobs, such as a headquarters for Prudential outside Philadelphia, and Daroff supported the architects. "But I never drove the design," she recalls, "and that became very frustrating and limiting. I saw that had we, the interior design staff, been able to have more influence early on, we could have made a building that was more efficient for the client and for the user."

In 1973 she left to set up her own firm, with a mission to offer a service that she called "Inside Out Design." By 1978 she had come a long way from her initial home-based operation with a few part-time associates, to establishing—within a forty-person firm servicing major law firms, corporations, restaurants, and hotels—an architectural division, focusing on life-safety and code-compliance issues. This step made Daroff Design Inc. one of the first interior design firms to offer the discipline of architecture in-house.

But it wasn't until 1981 that she moved up to a new level of efficiency by making James Rappoport executive vice-president and general manager of the company. "Jim articulated intellectually what I had been doing intuitively. We clarified the concept of Inside Out Design," says Daroff. Rappoport understood the investment that was needed to make this a unique service. The firm bought its own building and designed it to reflect the teamwork spirit. They renovated a 1920s' one-story, stand-alone industrial building by digging out the basement and creating a three-level space planned around a glass-roofed atrium. On the lower level, reached by a centrally positioned, red-painted metal stairway, senior staffers have glass-walled offices facing the atrium. The upper floors contain the open-area studios. To demonstrate confidence in state-of-the-art technology, the firm invested in computer management systems and CAD, hired computer programmers, established a middle-management training program, and helped overcome any staff resistance to these changes by employing an organizational psychologist. And it all worked. Staff turnover was reduced, in-house *esprit* was raised, and business boomed. "Up to then we had done everything manually, but we saw that it was essential to move into computers, as most of our clients wanted fast-track design," Daroff recalls. "With our new systems we had the capability of delivering a job in six, nine, or twelve months, when it had taken eighteen months to two years before."

Educated at Cornell and Columbia as an architect, Rappoport had long been interested in the interior design field, having been one of the founders of an important furniture firm, Atelier International, in the 1960s. He straddled two disciplines comfortably and helped to develop what by now has become a textbook method, known as the Workbook Approach, for both fields. The Daroff firm offers early consultation, before the architect comes into the project, to gather information about space requirements, learn about the client's business, and set out a quantitative and qualitative scenario.

"Cost-saving starts at the very beginning," says Daroff, "not just with the current lease negotiations but with understanding the long-term life-cycle costs, ten, twenty, and thirty years down the road." Many things must be considered, down to energy systems and wiring, building module, ratio of core to glass, and the social systems, such as community space. "We're not interested in building from the ground up. We do prearchitectural programs, planning the entire tenant fit-out, and like to work with the base building team. I don't want to knock architects, because one-third of my team is architects, but often an architect's desire to do architecture for the personal, internal satisfaction does not respond to the client's need and results in more lavish costs."

The Daroff consulting team got its service down to a fine art when a project came in from Revlon requiring the design of a New York facility of 330,000 square feet of space, consolidating twenty-five divisions and housing 1,000 people, to be completed on the fast track (within nine months) for relocation in the fall of 1989. This demanding exercise brought into play all the computerized production and design systems that the Daroff design team had learned to use. But because of the job's time limitations, they developed a workbook listing for different options of ceilings, lighting, computer flooring, workstations, and so forth. "We didn't want to wait until the time came to go out to bid on our project," explains Daroff, "and then find our design was over budget and had to be cut somewhere. That's what we call the 'silver spoons and paper plates syndrome,' and it's not good for the designer or the client."

Instead, the design team came up with a list of priced items, at three different budget levels—inexpensive, medium, and lavish—*before* design work was resolved. They then sat down with the client and the construction manager to reach decisions and get approvals. Thus, a consensus of macro and micro design elements was reached up front, not after the fact. The advantage of this Workbook Approach has since won Daroff other commissions and has begun to change clients' procedures. Even those with an established rigorous bidding process have overridden the practice to sign up with Daroff for the Workbook Approach to fast-track decision making.

Daroff believes that the firm, with its streamlined financial footing that includes a capital cost-recovery system, can continue to create innovative and outstanding design, which has always been the hallmark of her operation. Nothing is compromised to ensure that quality is maintained. Intricate marble inlays are designed for floors, metal inlays are beveled into custom furniture, stairways are fashioned with sandblasted glass, bronze, and mahogany, each unique to the specific site. And clients such as Comcast, Prudential, the Walt Disney Company, the Sagamore Resort Hotel, and major Philadelphia law firms have demonstrated their support. "You don't have to be big to be productive or profitable," she explains.

A selection of Daroff's work appears on pages 40 to 43.

Margo **Grant**

Top: Bank of America World Headquarters, San Francisco, California.

Above: Reception space, Gensler & Associates/Architects offices, New York City. Photograph by Nick Merrick, Hedrich-Blessing.

It is mid-afternoon and Margo Grant arrives at New York's JFK Airport from London. The next morning she leaves from LaGuardia for Walt Disney World, near Orlando, Florida, where she spends a day touring the new Team Disney headquarters, before heading out to the West Coast, to review the Team Disney headquarters in Burbank, California. She's back in New York within twenty-four hours, to check in at her office overlooking the Rockefeller Center skating rink in midtown Manhattan, the East Coast headquarters of Gensler & Associates/Architects (where she is vice president and managing principal), and despite the jet lag she's smiling. She has landed a plum job—the interiors for the new Team Disney headquarters near Paris, France—and after thirty years in the business, Grant still experiences a heady sense of exhilaration when a big project comes on board. "The Disney executives wanted a more budget-conscious approach for France," she reports, "after working with Michael Graves in California and Arata Isozaki in Florida. We were able to help them estimate the square footage they required with more accuracy, so that there was no wasted space."

With clients such as Goldman Sachs, Price Waterhouse, Mobil, Cravath Swaine & Moore, IBM, and McKinsey, Grant is perfectly attuned to the minds of power brokers and understands their conscientious regard for the bottom line. Business acumen, without question, has led to her remarkable position as the only woman among four managing principals of a design firm with 700 employees that bills $73 million annually, out of offices in San Francisco, Los Angeles, Houston, Washington, D.C., New York, and London. Yet while she can talk to clients in their own language, she is also a hands-on project designer who always has one job on her own drawing board and is likely to work on it during weekends, after the normal work week has been spent on client meetings and conferences with in-house management and staff.

Hard work, she stresses, is inevitably connected to growth. In 1979, after working for six years in Gensler's Houston office, she opened the New York office with just a secretary. By the end of that year she had a team of 15 people. Currently, she manages a staff of 120 in New York and 20 in London, where she spends one week in four, riding planes as others might ride subways. When she graduated from college in the late 1950s, such executive status for a woman would have been unthinkable. Born in Montana, part Black Foot Native American, Grant obtained both Bachelor of Science and Bachelor of Arts degrees in interior architecture from the University of Oregon—"not architecture," she emphasizes, "because as a female I was encouraged to be on the interiors side, where it was felt there would be more opportunity to get a job and succeed." With no job and no money after graduation, Grant moved to San Francisco, where she started out as a secretary. It was while working nights for Herman Miller that she was introduced to Alexis Yermakov, then a partner at Skidmore Owings & Merrill's San Francisco office. He liked her diligence and enthusiasm, found out that she could do renderings and make models, as well as type and organize, and hired her as his assistant. Grant stayed at SOM for thirteen years, learning from Yermakov and SOM's famous interior design associate, Davis Allen, rising to become director of the interior design department, with a staff of twenty people. An ability to organize, she believes, has been key to her progress. She notes that "too often there is chaos in a design office with missed deadlines and budget overruns," but many of her peers also point to her exceptionally strong sense of design, which has helped to create the "Gensler image" in terms of office style. This look is best exemplified in her own New York domain, with its golden wood-paneled reception area, black leather couches, window treatment of gridded wooden screens, and antique Persian carpet. From here, a wide wood-paneled corridor leads to the executive area, where Grant's offices are composed of two spaces, one with her drawing table and an antique damask-covered couch, and one with her Parsons-table desk and Brno chairs, divided by a gridded storage unit, containing some of her 350-piece collection of footstools. Grant often uses the exotic touch of a special antique carpet to create a tactile atmosphere within a strictly sleek and modern interior—something she learned from Davis Allen—and is fond of talking her clients into spending thousands of dollars on such items. "Even Arthur Gensler allowed me to spend lavishly for our own offices—that was a triumph!" she jokes.

Arthur Gensler's long-time appreciation for Grant is no secret, however. Observing her at SOM in the 1960s, when she was designing large-scale offices for Bank of America and Marine Midland, Gensler forecast that one day she would work for him. At the time, he was just starting his company, doing small tenant fit-outs, and was in no position to make her a competitive offer. But in 1973, when he landed the Pennzoil job in Houston, a 450,000-square-foot project in a world-class building designed by architect Philip Johnson, he offered her a contract she couldn't refuse. It was not just the thought of the project, and being in Texas during the time of the oil boom, but the way Gensler ran his business that appealed to Grant. Key employees were made shareholders in the company, and the management style was structured around participation. Even today, with a greatly expanded "family," Gensler still holds two meetings a year with his key people, who now number sixty-six, and one of these meetings is with spouses. This kind of commitment to participatory involvement is probably unique in the design profession and has laid the foundation for a company that Gensler plans to have live on for generations.

Grant strongly endorses this policy and has encouraged numerous young protégés whom she has hired to work for her, including the late Charles Pfister and Orlando Diaz-Azcuy, both of whom were to go out on their own and be named Designers of the Year in the 1980s, as well as be inducted into the *Interior Design* Hall of Fame. "It is something I learned from Dave Allen, when I worked with him on projects at SOM," she says. "I was only in my twenties, but he would still ask for my opinion. I truly believe in team spirit and team building."

It is a philosophy that many management experts and business schools espouse but few business operations practice in reality. In this instance, the value may be proven by the fact that when other competitors faltered in the downturn of 1990–91, Gensler expanded, both in billings and staff, partly by passing on this "caring credo" to its clients. The repeat work from long-standing clients who have grown accustomed to the Gensler management style kept the firm going. Ten years ago, Grant points out, when some business leaders talked about the quality and décor of a work environment being of importance to a new recruit, or having an employee dining facility that was more than a vending machine, they were met with skeptical reactions. Nowadays, this kind of employee consideration is more the rule than the reverse—certainly within large service corporations and law firms. Caring for employees has become central to a company's growth. But design services have altered, too. Grant also emphasizes that picking the carpet and the furniture accounts for only three percent of any given job. Moving and relocating hundreds of people, libraries, files, records, communication systems, and equipment, including computers, telephones, and air-conditioning, are factors added to the budget. Premoving lease advice, programming, and space-planning analysis are additional value-added services offered by sophisticated design firms.

In addition to providing office services, Grant sees the wisdom of moving into new markets. The Gap has recently become a client in Europe, demanding a chain of seventeen retail stores. Next on her target list for market penetration is the hospitality industry—specifically, major hotels. She is not intimidated by the thought because two of the world's most elegant hotels bear her stamp: the Mauna Kea Beach Hotel in Hawaii and the Wentworth in Sydney, Australia, both done when she was working for SOM in the mid-1970s. They are enduring examples of the kind of fine interior design she has practiced for three decades: modern yet eclectic, reflecting the character of the site and the personality of the client, and long-lasting. If there is anything Grant resists it's fashion: "I'm interested in style, not the style of design."

A selection of Grant's work appears on pages 44 to 47.

Kitty **Hawks**

It is five o'clock in the afternoon on Manhattan's Park Avenue, and Kitty Hawks has just arrived home from her office on 57th Street. She is having a cup of Earl Grey tea, her terrier at her feet. The apartment serves as her calling card and reflects the cosmopolitan taste that has helped her launch a very successful—and personal— interior design service. The sitting room is all white: white sofas, white pillows, white curtains. A scattering of antiques, potted plants, "important" mirrors, and selected pieces of contemporary furniture, including a bookcase designed by Ettore Sottsass, Jr., and a lamp by Philippe Starck, are contained within the white envelope. The floor is covered with a white-and-pastel dhurrie which she says was "the beginning of the room. I always like to start with the floor and go from there." There are art books piled everywhere, many of them monographs on leading architects and designers who are her "inspirations"—Tadao Ando, I. M. Pei, Issey Miyake, Arata Isozaki, and Andrée Putman.

Hawks has just returned from Los Angeles, where she has finished twenty offices for an important Hollywood talent agency. Like most of her clients, the agency prefers to remain nameless. Her work may not often be published, but her celebrated clients appreciate the lack of publicity surrounding the design of their houses and offices. She comes by her understanding of the idiosyncrasies of show-business personalities naturally: her father was Howard Hawks, the celebrated movie director, and her stepfather was Leland Hayward, the Broadway producer. Born in Los Angeles, Hawks spent her childhood in some of the most spectacular houses in Beverly Hills and Palm Springs, as well as other cities around the world—London, Paris, Biarritz, Gstaad, Monte Carlo. Her mother, Lady "Slim" Keith, who died in 1990, was known for her extraordinary vivacity and elegance and her picture-book life, spent among the rich and famous, which she chronicled in her best-selling autobiography, *Slim*. Wherever Hawks went with her mother, there was a special aura of style and taste. "The rooms I continually walked into were like magic," she recalls. "I remember a Billy Baldwin room based on a gray, white, and taupe batik fabric which was shirred on every wall. My mind is filled with rooms that gave you a sense of comfort and well-being and possessed luxury in the way they were detailed."

Hawks pursued architecture and design as a student at

the University of California, Los Angeles (UCLA), where her mentors were the then-dean Charles Moore, and such trendy California architects as Craig Hodgetts, Timothy Vreeland, Frank O. Gehry, Eric Owen Moss, and Robert Mangurian. "By the time I got to school, I was passionate about it," she relates. "It was like being in a candy store, seeing what they were doing, and asking them questions about it all." There was only one problem. She found that they all taught about structures and "the technical stuff," but little was taught about interiors. She also discovered "that architects did not trust interior designers, and that the reverse is also true. And I understand why. You can learn all about space planning, but you cannot learn the sensuality of decorative things."

Hawks did not finish her architecture degree, partly because her life changed and partly because she decided that she would be better at "inside rather than outside" issues. "It's really a question of whether you want to make buildings or rooms," she claims.

Coming to New York, she first fell into a job as creative director of the Perry Ellis fashion operation in the early 1980s. Then she became a vice president at the furniture firm Stendig International. In her fifteen-month tenure there, Hawks worked to re-focus the company's image, from one of 1960s' modern to one of 1980s' eclectic, in touch with the leading pacesetters in the design industry. She opened new showrooms designed by top designers and worked with international design celebrities such as Andrée Putman on new collections. It was a fertile period and a time for learning the last piece of the interiors puzzle: the commercial design market. Once that door was opened it broadened her knowledge and brought her face to face with the realization that interior design should be her full-time occupation. "Up until then, I just hadn't had the courage to do it. I always loved the process. I watched and I loved."

She elected to open a small studio with one assistant and decided to do "small amounts of good work rather than large amounts with a staff. I feel I don't need the pressure of a large organization to get personal satisfaction from my work," she says. Hawks believes that her architectural training helps her to work with her clients' architects. She understands what they are thinking, and she also knows what they are likely to forget. She always insists on getting involved in a project as early as possible, to avoid problems later, such as the discovery of windows that don't lend themselves to curtain rods or awkwardly shaped rooms that don't allow for comfortable furniture arrangements. In a recently completed job inside an I. M. Pei–designed building, the curve of an exterior wall was a challenge on the inside, requiring her to design custom furniture to fit the office spaces—to give the spaces a seamless look.

Hawks is insistent that she does not have a signature but rather an ability to change or adapt to a client's inclinations. She favors the work of stellar colleagues, such as Vicente Wolf, Sister Parish, Robert Currie, Renzo Mongiardino, and Stephen Sills, all of whom work mainly in the residential field and are renowned for their attitude toward comfort. "They all produce a

Above: Office for a talent agency, Los Angeles, California. Photograph by Michael Moran.

kind of effortless look, yet you know a mind has been at work. If you think about a door handle, then it's obvious someone else has thought about it before you. The yardstick for me is, can you put your feet up on the furniture and your head back and just relax? A room has to do what a body does," she remarks. "An interior has to accommodate life. You can't hide magazines, or keep a perfect pile on your office desk." For this reason, most of her work tends to be in what might be labeled "traditional" style, rather than strictly Modern, which she finds takes a great deal of mental discipline. And no space, she insists, should be a laboratory for experimentation: "If I were asked what impression I want to leave in my work, it would be peacefulness."

A selection of Hawks's work appears on pages 48 to 51.

Debra
Lehman-Smith

Outside the gracious dining room of the Hay-Adams Hotel in Washington, D.C., just a stone's throw from The White House, the sun is dappling the flower beds, creating a brilliant vista of blooms. Inside, hosting breakfast, Debra Lehman-Smith is talking about the revolution in her career: the founding (in March 1991) of Lehman-Smith Wiseman, which is headquartered a few blocks from the hotel.

The firm's new principal says she is relieved about her decision to go it alone, following a 12-year career at Skidmore Owings & Merrill. Her departure, she notes, was in part motivated by her frustration at not being made a full partner in the firm of approximately 1,500 which is managed by 25 to 40 full partners, depending on the number of offices operating at any time. She remarks, "I felt the firm had lost faith in interior design. I was very frustrated." Though Lehman-Smith had completed approximately twenty major interior design projects for a list of distinguished clients, including Sun Bank, Baker & Botts, Merrill Lynch, Marine Midland, and Tiffany & Company, every one of them the recipient of a design award, her career path stalled at the associate partner level.

Cutting bait dramatically, Lehman-Smith took twelve people from SOM's Washington office, including her new partner, Ken Wiseman, and James McLeish from SOM's Los Angeles office, along with two people from the Houston office, to set up her new shop. And not only staff walked with the two principals. She ensured proprietorship of seven projects on the boards, totaling one million square feet, including major buildings in progress in Colorado and San Diego, California, for the prestigious United States Olympic Committee.

Despite what must have been difficult negotiations, along with the pressure of establishing a new business, Lehman-Smith is smiling and declares she has never felt better or more relaxed. She has the support of some fifty clients ("I have always put my clients first and believed they were even more important than my firm.") and is convinced that she and her staff can provide a high-quality design service that is "progressive and pushes design to the limits." It will offer "one-stop shopping, including graphics, art selection, and technical services." It will also remain small. Lehman-Smith explains: "We don't want to be a 120-person firm. We'll be conservative about growing, because we want to keep up a team spirit. Our goal is simply to do great work."

If there is a special Lehman-Smith signature, it is her meticulous efforts to amalgamate beauty and efficiency. She credits her early mentors, the late Mel Hamilton, who was the first to hire her, and SOM's Rick Keating and Davis Allen, with introducing her to this extra dimension of creativity early in her career. (She joined SOM just after graduating from the University of Kentucky with a bachelor's degree in interior architecture in 1978.) Her portfolio demonstrates particular skill in convincing clients that they must go beyond the normal boundaries of interior design—that it is in their interests, in terms of future prosperity, to build corporate art collections and that this commitment translates into corporate image making at its most sophisticated level.

Ross Dixon & Masback, a law firm in Washington, D.C., for example, was persuaded to buy more than thirty pieces of French art deco furniture and objects, from chairs to fine glass pieces. "They wanted to buy George III," notes Lehman-Smith, "but we sat them down and tried to coerce them into doing something different and making a more farsighted investment. It worked. They paid $10,000 for six chairs and wound up investing $100,000 in total for a collection that will be worth many more times that in a few years."

Asked to name a highlight of her career, Lehman-Smith brings up Sun Bank in Orlando, Florida, a job that spanned six years in the 1980s and has received extensive publicity and numerous citations. The 350,000-square-foot project, comprising three buildings on a five-acre lot and accommodating 1,200 employees, was a "first" in demonstrating how a more residential approach could be successfully integrated into a commercial setting. A color palette of white, neutral beige, and teal blue is orchestrated throughout the main spaces, with a recurring grid theme, which is seen in lacquered walls, wood paneling in executive areas, etched-glass wall dividers, and shoji-like window screens.

As she does in all her projects, Lehman-Smith made a point of educating the client along the way, by standing up for what she was convinced was right. For Sun Bank, she held out for a collection of Biedermeier furniture—delicate, supremely elegant chairs and tables, which are positioned throughout the executive floor to give it an extraordinary caste of originality and taste. In the reception foyer, for example, silk-upholstered sofas with Fortuny silk pillows play against a marble floor, inset with a custom rug. Four Biedermeier side chairs upholstered in black silk provide points of punctuation. Another is pulled up in front of a writing table. Anyone entering this space would get the impression that the bank handles portfolios for very special clients and knows how to conduct its business with sophistication and quality. The decorations are complemented with works by contemporary artists, including George Segal, Robert Motherwell, David Hockney, Frank Stella, Larry Rivers, and Helen Frankenthaler. The Sun Bank art collection is also compiled into a handsome catalog that helps attune clients to the bank's commitment to the finest things in life and culture.

But creating luxurious, opulent environments is certainly not the Lehman-Smith credo. The designer is equally content working with modest budgets that require her to be exceptionally creative with materials, as was the case for the United States Olympic Committee. With a budget of $45 per square foot, including architecture and interiors, a range of inexpensive yet striking materials was employed: vibrant colors, sealed concrete floors, yachting cables, and harp wire woven in an overhead grid pattern instead of a regular ceiling treatment. "We took the same approach, creating an elegance as if we were doing something at $100 per square foot," she emphasizes. "But we pushed the edges a bit more."

The firm is working on several other projects for this client: the San Diego Olympic Training Center on 150 acres contains fifty-four buildings for more than twenty sports; the Colorado Springs Olympic Training Center includes a fifty-meter indoor pool and gymnasiums for ten sports; the Visitor Center and Headquarters and Command Centers in Albertville, France, and Barcelona, Spain, built for the 1992 winter and summer games; and the renovation of the Lake Placid Olympic Training Center for winter sports practice. The thrust of this effort is to encourage more young Americans to enter the coaching process for the Olympics and thereby gain more recognition for American athletes in this four-year global meeting. Image making for the Olympic Committee is part of her brief; it includes everything in the facilities, down to the dinnerware, which is designed in conjunction with Tiffany.

Having worked in Houston, New York, and Washington, Lehman-Smith sees great potential in locating her firm's headquarters in the nation's capital. First, it is an international city, with a global outreach. Second, its business is not just corporate but includes government work, and she would very much like to work on a government buildings. And third, "It has a heart."

Above: Lobby, Sun Bank, Orlando, Florida, a Skidmore Owings & Merrill project. Photograph by Hedrich-Blessing.

A selection of Lehman-Smith's work appears on pages 52 to 55.

STEVE SCHRAM

Dian **Love**

T he offices of Payette Associates in Boston, where Dian Love is a senior designer in the interior design department, do not appear to be lacking projects for the 1990s. This is because the firm specializes in segments of the design industry that are predicted to be buoyant during the decade: health care and medical research. The walls are papered with impressive footprints for projects, including two flagship buildings at Duke University, with budgets of $30 and $40 million; a building at New York University with a budget of $150 million; an outpatient center at Baltimore's Johns Hopkins Medical Center comprising 420,000 square feet of examination rooms, doctors' offices, and waiting rooms; and corporate projects for American Cyanamid and Merck.

Payette Associates is recognized as a leader in the field of medical-research design. The firm's understanding of this particular segment's needs is indicated in the Duke University buildings, which provide scientists with almost as much "interactive" space as they do "bench" space for high-tech work, which has moved away from heavy chemical experimentation to computer- and laser-oriented tasks. Experience has shown that informal meeting areas are where "breakthroughs" are very often made—in the exchange of scientific data and in "chalkboarding" ideas. The designers at Payette have even built in stairways for the occupants to use from floor to floor, which offer them the chance to meet casually in passing and stop for those all-important "chats."

"Our work is all about making interiors more effective," says Love, who is in the satisfying position of having joined the two strands of her career—design and environmental psychology—at this 150-person East Coast firm. "We think about how people connect visually to the institution, bring cohesiveness to a facility. I find I am being pushed to provide the best information on products, materials, finishes. At the same time, we must design in enormous flexibility. Construction costs so much today that a building must be readily reassigned to new activities, without a major renovation, during the course of its use. Incredibly, forty-five percent of the cost of a space goes into its mechanical systems. Research labs are the most expensive buildings that we have created in our society. They are also the key to our

Above: Residence on Walden Pond, Concord, Massachusetts. Photograph by David Pollack.

future, in terms of genetic engineering and finding cures for cancer and AIDS."

To Love, the design commitment goes well beyond the task of creating a functional, pleasing environment. Her objective is to create spaces that provoke the occupants into considering whether they are asking the right questions in their research. This is where her background in behavioral psychology comes into play. Love grew up in Indiana and received an undergraduate degree in interior design from Purdue University. She went on to get her Master of Fine Art degree from the University of Michigan, where she also pursued doctoral studies in Environmental Psychology and Behavior at the School of Architecture. "I'm afraid that the behavioral component has been lost in much of the design work that goes on today, " she remarks. "It's an uphill battle sometimes to convince clients of the therapeutic value of the environment. Yet time and again, we have have proof that heart, soul, and spirit participate in the healing process and are essential to the medical field. So it should be recognized that these are essential components in all kinds of spaces."

Love's first job was at the University Hospital at the University of Michigan, where she established a program of interior design for the one million square feet of space on the medical campus. It was there that she began to consider the designer's responsibility in providing an environment that emphasizes recovery and wellness. A few years later, working on the massive Detroit Receiving Hospital, a joint venture of William Kessler Associates of Detroit, Eberhard Zeidler of Toronto, and the Giffels engineering firm, which included a city-owned trauma hospital, a university outpatient clinic, and a teaching facility, Love was on the interior design team that helped the project win an *Interiors* award. The awards jury cited the designers' concern for color and natural light as a remarkable accomplishment in a field "so often dominated by grim and utilitarian structures." For once, they noted, architecture had gone beyond the norm, liberating dark corridors, creating attractive nurses' stations, and using graphics and artworks to enliven spaces. The complex was concerned not just with putting all the necessary elements in place; it was sensitive first and foremost to the patients.

Love's next career stop was at the offices of Gunnar Birkets in Birmingham, Michigan, a firm whose masterly effects with natural light helped her to develop a deeper understanding of this particularly important design element. In 1980 she was offered a position too challenging to refuse: a professorship at the Rhode Island School of Design, with the assignment to start an interior design department. With her energy and drive, she succeeded in establishing a department with sixty students and five faculty within four years.

However, a keen desire to get back into the practice of design took her, in 1984, to the Boston firm of Cambridge Seven, where she participated with the firm's architectural team on interiors for several major buildings, including EPCOT Center near Orlando, Florida, and the Tennis Hall of Fame at the historic Casino in Newport, Rhode Island. But when Payette offered her a job in 1990, she jumped at the opportunity to move wholeheartedly into the health-care design field. Because the firm has so many projects in progress, it can afford to take on small *pro bono* jobs that are particularly satisfying, both to the office and to the local community. One such recent project was Easler House, an AIDS hospice in Gloucester, Massachusetts.

Love and colleague Vance Hosford set a new standard at Easler House, a model that any care-providing organization can follow. They succeeded in creating a truly homelike environment, embracing the sense of both security and freedom associated with a residence, in contrast with the restrictions of the conventional prison-type hospitals or health-care facilities, where the objective is to depersonalize, sanitize, and homogenize the environment. Paneled walls, handpainted wallpapers, bookshelves, adjustable wooden desk-tables, and comfortable upholstered chairs were all introduced to encourage a sense of dignity and self-esteem in the residents. Such an environment, Love points out, is suitable not only for AIDS victims but also for people recovering from substance abuse.

Equally challenging to Love and her colleagues is the need to establish new design standards for the elderly, those who do not require nursing care but need help in living in a dignified manner as they reach their eighties and beyond—an increasingly common phenomenon nowadays. A typical recent Payette project was a 100-unit facility for the elderly with common areas for shared activities, similar to a hotel, and with private spaces for living. Love has found that for those with impaired vision, the floor plane can provide guidelines for moving from space to space, "delineating the edges of the rooms, helping to mark out the figure-ground relationships." She adds that "images must be set out in space." Also important, however, is providing a sense of personal control —by allowing people to control the air, light, and temperature in their own spaces. "These are the subtle, subconscious elements that people *do* notice; they have a major effect on whether people feel comfortable or nervous, and thus affect their state of mind."

Love feels she is in exactly the right place at the right time, a fortunate circumstance that many other designers— male and female—may envy, but her story is an example of a philosophy of attention that leads to an end result of satisfaction for the user, rather than preoccupation with the superficial decoration and finishing of surfaces.

A selection of Love's work appears on pages 56 to 59.

TOM MCCLUSKEY

Eva **Maddox**

Above: AGI showroom interior, designed for the 1991 Neocon exhibition at the Chicago Merchandise Mart. Photograph by Darwin Davidson.

E very year, with astonishing regularity, the offices of Eva Maddox Associates in Chicago reach a state of frenzy in late May and early June. There is nothing quite like it, because there is nothing quite like Neocon, the annual furniture trade show held at the world's largest building, the Chicago Merchandise Mart, located just a few blocks from the designer's headquarters in a renovated warehouse. Maddox is president of this firm, in business since 1975, which captures the lion's share of new showroom design for the Neocon show. In some years the firm has executed as many as ten new showroom interiors, all of which had to be completed at the same time, with the owners clamoring for the principal designer's attention.

Maddox's record (fifty-plus showrooms between 1981 and 1991) in this area of design feeds on its success. She started winning showroom awards in 1981, with a breakthrough design for a wallcovering manufacturer, for whom she created an all-black background wall on which she displayed tiny, colorful swatches of the product—quite unlike the traditional method of showing off fabrics in a cumbersome, swinging-panel system. From that moment on, it was acknowledged that the Maddox concept of marketing was startlingly different—but that it worked most effectively.

Maddox was the first to get carpet samples out of the "waterfall" display syndrome into more imaginative, sensual environments. Fiber manufacturers' showrooms suddenly became theatrical experiences, with tactile and psychological resonances allied to pulsing music and light. Even mundane architectural wall systems were somehow magically transformed with her creative solutions. The originality of the showrooms' designs generated publicity, which in turn pulled in the customers and sold the products.

Furthermore, the Maddox method did not inevitably require a big-time budget. While she could express the stature and impact of a major office-furniture company like Haworth if she was given a million dollars to spend, she could also create a memorable and effective environment, through the use of strong graphics, video, and color, when allocated a bare-bones budget of $50,000 by a small seating company such as AGI or Charlotte. One particularly good example of a successful low-budget design was a black-and-white showroom for AGI, with sofas lined up cinema-style before a screen showing black-and-white "oldies," and with posters of film stars displayed on the walls. Tickets were sold at the door, encouraging passersby to step in and see the show—engaging them in an instant relationship with the manufacturer's products.

According to Maddox, the challenge of showroom design is similar to that of newspaper journalism. Quality and originality matter, of course, but above all the product must, like a newspaper, get out on time. Often a showroom project must be completed, from initial concept to ribbon-cutting ceremony, in just 120 days. With such strict operational deadlines, the in-house design team at Eva Maddox Associates, which numbers around twenty people, has learned to operate with exceptional efficiency, a skill that it is able to put to use with other clients as well. About half of the firm's work is in the showroom field, and the remainder is in retail and corporate-office planning and design.

The firm's success was quickly noted by its peers in the Chicago area, as were its sophisticated sales techniques, specifically that of offering "packages" to showroom manufacturers via direct marketing. And though, according to Maddox, many of her contemporaries look on marketing as a "primary evil," her methodology and expertise gained her academic acceptance from the department of architecture at the University of Illinois. The chairman of the department, architect Stanley Tigerman, offered her an unusual opportunity—to teach interior architecture with a substantive message beyond the usual "F F & E" (fixtures, furnishings, and equipment).

The invitation presented Maddox with an intriguing challenge—to present a theory of interior architecture as a distinctively separate discipline—and one to which she was more than ready to respond. She remarks that "interiors has a tendency to be a 'boudoir' discipline, because it's in a box. But there should be no boundaries. As designers, we have learned to create patterns of design, patterns that bring vision, synthesis, and solutions, to the extent that maybe we've forgotten what we really *need* to do, and what we should be doing."

Her university course introduced students to three concepts synthesized into a working model for the design process: parallels, patterns, and positioning. The concepts draw upon design and architectural principles and are interrelated with scientific, physical, and anthropological models. Her definitions are as follows: *Parallels* are the concurrent lines of events and thoughts that occur in time—for example, the celebration of art, the move from an industrial to a postindustrial society, the freedom movement, the emerging awareness of ecology. *Patterns* represent the repetitive models that establish perceptions of society and our evolution in terms of history. Patterns express our culture—in relation to industrial product models, political models, psychological models, and archeological models. They represent memories that are brought to bear in the design process at any scale, from the spoon to the city. *Positioning* is the resolution of the interaction of parallel thought and pattern, which propels the resulting idea forward. Positioning occurs when history and history in the making

have been observed, patterns have been learned from, and a new process has been effected. Evidence of the success of this new, ten-week academic course was immediate, with several students winning recognition in the annual Chicago chapter AIA awards program in the first year.

With the Maddox philosophy, issues of individual designer style are forgotten, because there is no single style. "Design becomes an enhancement," Maddox says. And she is not afraid to admit that her own lack of a signature design style has lost her firm some projects. She feels, however, that "this philosophy keeps a designer fresh, because you are always looking for new ways to do something. You don't just offer a label." Re-education along such lines, she believes emphatically, is what's needed for everyone engaged in design today.

Born and brought up in Tennessee, Maddox was reared in a household where building and education were integral: her father was a contractor, and her mother worked in the public school system. From an early age, she was cutting apart wallpaper books to make paper dolls' clothes. Her predilection for systems and order led her to become a math major at the University of Tennessee. The leap into design resulted from a reflection that mathematics and architecture enjoyed a close relationship, and that her talent for three-dimensional thinking could be exploited through continuing her education at the University of Cincinnati, in the department of architecture and interior design. She graduated with a degree in interior architecture which, even with the hands-on, highly respected, UC coop program, she says, did not adequately prepare her for the real-life experiences that were to come.

Asked to name a mentor who has helped her most in her career, Maddox chooses two men, not from the disciplines of architecture or design but from the world of business: Jim Allen of Booze Allen ("He taught me that design cannot be pushed to the client, and I did not appreciate the client's side before I learned it from him.") and Professor Charles Handy, author of the book *The Age of Unreason* (Harvard Business School Press, 1990), a guide to understanding "discontinuous" change. ("He helped me to move my thinking forward.") But Allen, she points out, is an enlightened client, one of a rare breed that educates itself on the value of investment in design. Understanding that shortfalls in this designer-client relationship are a result of lack of knowledge on both sides, she maintains, led her to conclude that this discrepancy could only be modified by education much earlier in the learning process. To this end, Maddox has spent a good deal of time during the last few years developing a now-patented children's educational system that is to be marketed at retail for parents to buy and teachers to adopt. The system, called "Eve's Kinder Garden," offers early environmental awareness. "I feel this will take me into a new phase of my career," says Maddox. "It's a Big Idea and might have phenomenally far-reaching effects."

A selection of Maddox's work appears on pages 60 to 63.

Right, top and bottom: The renovation of the Blanchard Howard Bartlett Theater at Hobart and William Smith Colleges, Geneva, New York, offered a sensitive brief: to refit the room as a modern performance space reflecting the increased seriousness of the college's commitment to theater, while not compromising the building's historical attributes. Side boxes were installed, derived from nineteenth-century music rooms, to define a new central seating or performance area in addition to the stage. The introduction of a catwalk system to provide safe and flexible support for lighting focused attention on the room's remarkable decorative ceiling brackets. The room's historic woodwork was restored and carefully lit to highlight its painted escutcheons. Photographs by Norman McGrath.

Opposite: In a functional, double-height studio addition to a beach house at Gay Head on Martha's Vineyard, the vernacular style of the architecture provided a shell for an eclectic selection of furnishings. Photograph by Norman McGrath.

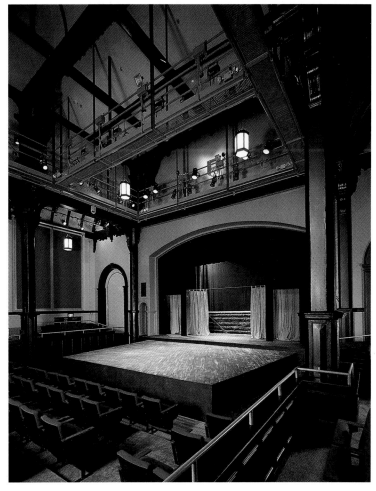

Left, top and bottom: In a special project for Interiors, *cosponsored by* Working Woman, *Armstrong explored the office-design vocabulary for the executive woman. A strong palette of hunter green, gray, yellow, and lilac expressed a move away from traditional pastels. The four-part space included working and conference zones, informal meeting spaces, and a service area for coats and catering. All the built-ins were custom designed. An open grid system overhead was rotated as a counterpoint to the conventional box-shaped space. Photographs by Roger Bester.*

Opposite: In a Manhattan penthouse renovation for Charles Schwartz and his wife, Nancy Drosd, a painter, the entire space was gutted and replanned. Much consideration was given to the couple's distinguished collection of paintings and photographs. A new two-flight grand stair was installed to link two residential floors and a painting studio. Built on either side of the staircase was a gallery, lofty enough to accommodate an eleven-foot-long work by Robert Rauschenberg and a nineteenth-century post office counter. Photograph by Norman McGrath.

Above: An octagonally shaped conference/dining room at United Business Interiors, Los Angeles, occupies the center of an unusual "open plan" executive area. Doorways open on three sides to surrounding offices. Furnishings, such as the Mario Bellini–designed seating and the table designed by Massimo and Lella Vignelli, reflect the client's desire to furnish the space with the most renowned pieces of modern furniture design. Photograph by Alexander Vertikoff.

Left: With little natural light available in the space, a golden glow of indirect light was provided in the reception area at United Business Interiors. Flooring is beige limestone; walls were sponged in a parchmentlike tone. Photograph by Alexander Vertikoff.

Opposite: A grand scale pervades the lobby of Citicorp's international private banking facility, in a Skidmore Owings & Merrill–designed building in Los Angeles. Under the twenty-one-foot-high ceiling, granite floors, mahogany teller counters, leather seating, and bronze detailing were deemed appropriate for the type of business conducted here. Photograph by Jon Miller, Hedrich-Blessing.

Opposite and right: The offices of La Opinion, a Spanish-language newspaper, occupy 60,000 square feet in a renovated 1930s downtown Los Angeles building. Circular themes are utilized in the imaginatively designed, low-budget ($28 per square foot) space. The reception area, opposite, is topped by a lowered cylinder, its cut-outs admitting light and echoing the circular carpet inserts. Western Heroes, a painting by Hispanic artist Eloy Torrez, hangs above the receptionist's workstation. In the open-plan newsroom, top right, low-height drywall partitions are painted green and edged with yellow plastic laminate to establish a feeling of permanent architecture. Ceilings are punctuated with large acrylic lighting disks, bottom right, to illuminate the computer-equipped reporters' workstations. Photographs by Alexander Vertikoff.

Above: Daroff's crisp sense of elegance pervades the boardroom of the Capital Blue Cross offices in Harrisburg, Pennsylvania. Photograph by Tom Crane.

Above: A sweeping stairway serves as a sculptural element in the lobby of the Prudential Eastern Home Office, Ft. Washington, Pennsylvania. Photograph by Wolfgang Hoyt.

Right: A freeform concrete reception desk greets visitors to the USG showroom at the International Design Center, New York (IDCNY) in Long Island City. The company's interior building products—ceilings and wall systems—are displayed throughout the space. Photograph by Norman McGrath.

Above: The soaring guest registration area at Disney's Dixie Landings Resort in Lake Buena Vista, Florida, offers a slick interpretation of Southern vernacular design. Photograph by Elliott Kaufman.

Right: Daroff was chosen to renovate the lobby and reception area of the Contemporary Resort Hotel at Disney World, near Orlando, Florida. The interior elegantly updates the 1960s-style architecture of the building. Photograph by Elliott Kaufman.

Right: Grant's modern approach is apparent in an executive office at the Newsweek offices in New York City. A lacquered Parsons-style table serves as a desk, surrounded by cane bucket chairs. A large, frameless glass wall provides a view to the secretarial area and a private conference and dining room beyond. Photograph by Jaime Ardiles-Arce.

Below right: Grant's office, in the New York headquarters of Gensler and Associates/Architects at Rockefeller Center, is a two-part space: an informal conference area leads to the managing principal's work area, furnished with a drawing board and a comfortable antique sofa. The wall dividing the spaces contains niches in which some pieces from Grant's extensive collection of antique footstools are displayed. Photograph by Nick Merrick, Hedrich-Blessing.

Opposite: Traditional elegance was required in the design for the Washington, D.C., offices of Steptoe & Johnson, a prominent legal firm. The black-and-white marble floors of the elevator lobby lead to a reception area. Beyond the gridded glass wall is a conference space. Furnishings were selected from the client's extensive collection of antiques. Photograph by Jaime Ardiles-Arce.

Above: At Covington & Burling, a Washington, D.C., law firm, the client's collection of art, antique rugs, and furniture dictated the style of the public spaces. The main reception area is reached through elegant transparent glass doors. Wood floors and crown and base moldings help to provide an authentic envelope for the furnishings. Photograph by Jaime Ardiles-Arce.

Opposite: The several floors of Cravath, Swaine & Moore's offices in New York City are linked by a dramatic internal staircase. The connection enables the giant law firm to reduce the number of reception areas to one for every third floor. Photograph by Nick Merrick, Hedrich-Blessing.

Above: A Los Angeles talent agency office is carefully configured to enhance the effect of the curving walls in a building designed by architect I. M. Pei. The desk was custom designed by Hawks. Photograph by Michael Moran.

Opposite: Hawks respected the existing architectural character of a duplex apartment on Manhattan's West Side. The two-story space is anchored with an antique Persian carpet. English furniture is placed to provide a variety of seating and conversation areas. Photograph by Oberto Gili, courtesy of the Condé Nast Publications, Inc.

Above and right: For a designer showcase house in New York City, the designer created the "Hawk's Nest," an ideal study. The walls are covered in cork for a textural effect; the floor is enriched with a Turkestan carpet. Hawks found the eccentric bird cage, once owned by fashion designer Coco Chanel, on an antiques-gathering trip. Photographs by Michael Moran.

Opposite: This elegantly simple stairway in a Manhattan apartment was designed for a working couple who asked for a "monotone" look. The "quiet" color scheme of the walls and ceiling serves as an appropriate background for a serene Audubon artwork and a metal lighting fixture. Photograph by Oberto Gili, courtesy of the Condé Nast Publications, Inc.

Above: In the offices of Vinson &
Elkins, a prominent Dallas, Texas,
law firm, period furnishings have
been successfully used within contemporary surroundings. Granite
floors, which are seen in the street-
level public foyer, are repeated in
the waiting room, furnished with
an antique oriental rug, shield-back
armchairs, and contemporary sofas
and occasional tables. Silk-
upholstered walls and sleek glass
doors provide a subtle sense of
luxury appropriate for this type
of client. Photograph by Hedrich-
Blessing.

Right: A lacquered staircase links the floors of the Washington, D.C., offices of Baker & Botts. Photograph by Nick Merrick, Hedrich-Blessing.

Below: The design of the 50,000-square-foot office space for Baker & Botts respects the architecture of the I. M. Pei–designed building in which it is located, and alludes to the classical vocabulary that characterizes the architecture of Washington, D.C. A grand marble-floored "rotunda" reception area, with eight stylized fluted columns, creates a formal air. The paving pattern of the floor is mirrored on the ceiling. Photograph by Nick Merrick, Hedrich-Blessing.

*Opposite, top: In the lobby of the
Texas Commerce Bank, Dallas, the
grid pattern of the paved marble
floors is echoed on the ceiling
plane. Fluted Indiana limestone
walls add to the effect of security
and permanence related to the history of bank design. Photograph by
Jon Miller, Hedrich-Blessing.*

*Opposite, bottom: Lehman-Smith
works to convince clients that good
design benefits their employees as
much as it does their customers.
Her back-of-the-house areas are
as finely detailed as public spaces.
The cafeteria at the Sun Bank
headquarters in Orlando, Florida,
is a model example, with its granite
floor, clean stainless-steel finishes,
and decorative lighting scheme.
Photograph by Jon Miller,
Hedrich-Blessing.*

*Above: A meeting room at the Texas
Commerce Bank is impeccably
orchestrated. Rows of upholstered
armchairs, a graceful front table,
and a classic landscape painting
contribute to the elegance of the
setting. Photograph by Jon Miller,
Hedrich-Blessing.*

Above: The ballroom in the Atlantic City Convention Center, home of the annual "Miss America" pageant each year, was reborn in a 1980s renovation undertaken while Love was associated with Cambridge Seven Associates. The best of its 1929 art deco-style details were preserved. Photograph by Thorney Lieberman.

Left: A major entrance corridor at the Atlantic City Convention Center was upgraded, with a flamed and polished granite floor, cove lighting, and columns sheathed in blue-green fiberglass. Love worked with lighting designer Howard Brandston on the project. Photograph by Thorney Lieberman.

Opposite, top: A patient room at the Detroit Receiving Hospital was equipped with a corridor-view window partition, allowing the nursing staff to see patients, and giving patients the option to view hallway activity. Photograph by Timothy Hursley/Balthazar Korab Ltd.

Opposite, bottom: Colorful seating for adults and children was installed in a light-filled waiting area of the radiology department at the Wayne State Clinics Building, part of the Detroit Receiving Hospital complex. Photograph by Timothy Hursley/Balthazar Korab, Ltd.

Above: A custom-designed pull-down desk and bookshelf unit adds warmth to a patient room at the Easler House AIDS hospice in Gloucester, Massachusetts. A hand-painted wallpaper adds to the residential feeling. Photograph by Paul Ferrino.

Left: A former attic space has been put to use as a counseling and meeting room at Easler House. The facility is a model of residential-style institutional design. Its home-like appearance was deemed an appropriate environment for people who need emotional and psychological support. Photograph by Paul Ferrino.

Right: Du Pont's design trade showroom at the Pacific Design Center in West Hollywood, California, combines bold graphics and colors—in tune with West Coast design attitudes. The focus is on commercial and residential carpet (made of the company's Antron™ fiber) as a fashion statement. Photograph by Hedrich-Blessing.

Below right: Cynthia, a retail sportswear store in Chicago, was designed to attract the young customer with its clublike configuration, sophisticated color scheme, and overall kinetic appearance. The shop's plan offers a central circulation path, flanked by a series of symmetrically placed mini-boutiques. Photograph by Darwin Davidson.

Opposite: For the Chicago offices of Hawthorne Realty, Maddox converted a "nondescript" brownstone, preserving the best of its historical elements while transforming the infrastructure—ducts, columns, stairwells, and beams—into unexpected decorative devices. The playfulness of the design matches the firm's creative business style. Photograph by Hedrich-Blessing.

Left: In a region where Frank Lloyd Wright is an architectural hero, Maddox's geometrical detailing on the stairway of the University of Illinois, Chicago Circle Campus Student Commons is evocative of Wright's aesthetic. Photograph by Nick Merrick, Hedrich-Blessing.

Below left: The Atlanta conference center of Collins & Aikman reflects the subdued, yet up-to-date character of the company's floorcovering division. The interior is reflective of the theoretical principles of the Vienna Secessionists, who touted the integration of all elements of an interior, while also embracing their pared-down aesthetic. Photograph by Hedrich-Blessing.

Opposite: Eva and Lynn Maddox's own Lake Shore Drive residence in Chicago offers a 1920s-vintage vaulted ceiling in the foyer. Its ornamental plasterwork is highlighted via custom lighting effects. The gallery-like spaces are sparely furnished, though filled with an impressive collection of contemporary paintings, sculpture, and handcrafted pieces. Photograph by Steve Hall, Hedrich-Blessing.

Martha **Burns**

PURISTS

The traditional trappings of beauty and

comfort are the concerns of those designers

categorized as Purists. They work in a variety of

historical styles and are well versed in the

language of antique furnishings and period

detailing. Purists also respect the revivalist

attitudes of recent times—the Postmodernist

bent for ornamentation, decoration,

and vivid color.

Martha Burns's résumé lists eleven different jobs in twenty years, which is more than most of her peers can chalk up. But turning to a metaphor for explanation, she says, "I'm a textile weaver and I have been weaving my way through experiences ever since I first got into architecture." Like so many artists, once Burns graduated from Yale University with a master's degree in architecture, she put aside her work on the loom to take up a less risky career as an architect and interior designer. But her work as an interior designer has focused strongly on the tactile and psychological dimensions of a space.

Burns saw a felicitous opportunity for an environmentally oriented career while an undergraduate at Newton College in Boston (she earned a bachelor's degree in fine arts and mathematics, with an emphasis on tapestry weaving, in 1972), where she had a roommate who was studying psychology. "It turned out that it was possible to measure environmental impact on psychiatric patients, and I was fascinated to find out that things like color, light, texture, and space could make a difference in a person's behavior and mental outlook. I started investigating, with a grant from the Cabot Foundation, to implement an environmental design project to effect a physical, visual, and psychological change at the Boston University–Boston City Hospital Child Psychiatric Clinic." This project was followed by a renovation of the pediatrics ward at Baltimore Hospital, while she was an intern for the United States government during the summer of 1974. By this time she was engaged in graduate work at the Yale School of Architecture, studying under her professor and mentor, Charles Moore, who was dean of the school at the time. "It was fashionable to have guest lecturers at Yale who talked about drawings and the sculptural quality of architecture, but I always kept asking, 'What about the people?' " she recalls. "It was not a concern in the core program at Yale, but I found out about an elective, the environmental design program, which to me was much more to the point."

The faculty members of this program, including Don Watson, Walter Harris, Gary Winkel, and Bob Frew, connected her to a team of psychologists at the City University of New York, who were coordinating research on the effects of the environment on psychiatric treatment, with reference to one important building: The Bronx Children's Psychiatric Facility, a much-publicized and praised (by architecture and design critics) building completed in 1974 by Richard Meier. As elegant and sculptural as the building was, it did not function well for its inhabitants, who were predominantly minority tenement dwellers. Its gleaming aluminum-paneled exterior and monochromatic interiors of gray, white, and stainless steel were failures from a therapeutic standpoint—that is, they did not have a positive effect on the patients' mental health. Inquiries were launched, and reports showed that the building lacked color, sympathetic texture, and good lighting. Worse, the organization of individual rooms made patients feel isolated, and the public spaces, such as the swimming pool and cafeteria, did not define individual territory sufficiently. "It was altogether too cold, colorless, and impersonal," says Burns. "And it was totally inappropriate for Bronx slum children who had been sleeping on the floor, with six to a room."

Specific research demonstrated that circulation should be clear and direct, with proper lighting, color, and items of interest to break the monotony. White, sterile, poorly lit (or too brightly lit), long corridors are intimidating and disorienting. "Light," says Burns, "is a major element in the manipulation of space as it creates color, shade, and shadow, and should provide windows to reality (the outside world), but glazing should not be so extensive that it creates a fishbowl effect, which can be terrifying to some people—also very harmful."

The physiology of color, defined in the psychiatric context, can be applied successfully in everyday life, Burns notes. Orange may impair one's sense of security, gray may stimulate creativity, while pale blue tends to encourage calm and tranquility and reduce excitement. Yellow may be bright and cheerful to some, but to many it suggests anxiety. Pink can diminish aggressive behavior, but red tends to encourage excitement and stimulation. Green generally has a tranquil effect. White can create anxious, negative behavior.

Upon graduation, Burns took her architectural social consciousness to federal agencies in Washington, D.C., where she developed managerial and administrative capabilities. By 1980 she was out on the West Coast, engaged in the upcoming 1984 Olympic Games program, eventually finding a place as a staff member of the Los Angeles Olympics Organizing Committee, with responsibility for eight of the twenty-three sites, including the rowing and canoeing venues and the equestrian facility. Expanding the design team along the way from 25 people to 2,500, Burns got her first taste of male opposition to a woman architect, and came close to filing a discrimination suit against the construction management. She recalls: "I felt perfectly comfortable on a construction site, but they clearly didn't want me there. It was the first time I felt held back." Fortunately, Peter Ueberroth, the Olympic Games commission-

Above: Cocktail lounge, Embassy Suites Hotel, New York City. Photograph by Peter Paige.

er, came to her aid. "He had great respect for design in terms of the final product," notes Burns. "He wanted to make sure the money was invested properly for the future and that the games would not produce sites that became white elephants."

After the Games were over, sensing that interior design was coming into focus in architectural firms, Burns took a job at the New York office of Hellmuth, Obata & Kassabaum. As a project manager from 1984 to 1987, she had her first experience in a firm where management, design, and production were separate disciplines, which she found "very difficult." She moved to her present job as design principal at Fox & Fowle Architects, where, as director of interiors, she administers work on a totally different basis. "There is no interiors department here," she says. "Everyone works on everything; we are united in one studio. What we have established is that some people have more of an inclination to do interiors and want to take the time to understand shade and shadow, color and texture, detailing, lighting, and furnishings. Most young architects haven't got a clue what it is all about, they have no training or education, and my greatest satisfaction is to hear them say that they realize how much they don't know."

As an architect, Burns sees the level of integration that Fox & Fowle has been able to accomplish as extraordinary: "In most big architectural firms, interiors is seen as inferior work, but we have been able to dispense with that idea. Our team understands the level of quality in a space, and that the success of it hangs on the environmental aspects of color, lighting, quality of air, volume—all the intangible elements that comprise an interior—even whether the furniture arrangement is intimidating or welcoming."

Burns is insistent that the philosophy is put into practice whatever the job—be it the Embassy Suites Hotel on Times Square, the Indian Mission to the United Nations, or the headquarters of Local 32B-J Service Employees International Union, all recently completed in New York—and whatever the size—ranging from a 500,000-square-foot convention center in Jakarta, Indonesia, to a 1,600-square-foot hairdressing salon. "Diversity," she notes, "keeps a team fresh. The more varied the work, the more it helps us to solve problems."

Recently, Burns returned to her loom, working in the studio of textile designer Jack Lenor Larsen, listening to his ideas, and articulating them in woven fabrics. She sees this reintegration of art into architecture as adding an all-important dimension to her interior design work. "We come up with new fabrics that I can integrate into projects. I recently wove a bubble effect in nylon yarn that is extraordinarily architectural and could be introduced—even into an office."

A selection of Burns's work appears on pages 80 to 83.

MARY NOBLE OURS

Lee Foster-Crowder

Shortly after the 1991 Persian Gulf War, when Kuwait was a focus of attention for the design community because of the reconstruction going on following the military devastation, Lee Foster-Crowder got on the telephone in her Washington, D.C., office to find out how she could get a piece of the action. Unfazed by the news that the government was considering only large design firms for commissions (hers numbers twelve people), she nevertheless asked for all the forms and procedures for entering the bidding process. As she considered ways to circumvent the bureaucracy, her thoughts turned to joint-venturing. Through serendipitous connections, she allied herself with the Chicago firm of Perkins & Will, and the two firms proceeded to bid on the renovation of Kuwait's conference center—which Perkins & Will had built in the first place during the 1980s. In such a situation, a small firm might easily have been gobbled up by the larger one, with its superior administrative resources and executive knowledge, but Foster-Crowder is a person to be reckoned with, and she lost no time in reminding Perkins & Will that she had initiated the proposal in the first place. She took the lead in the entire process, with the backing of the Army Corps of Engineers.

That Foster-Crowder can hold her own against an architectural Goliath and get through the maze of political red tape that goes along with government-sponsored projects is a function of her having two personas: one as an artist, architect, and designer; the other as a communicator with leanings toward law, politics, and journalism. After graduation from Wake Forest University in North Carolina, with a bachelor's degree in political science and the history of education, she first taught high school, before deciding to return to North Carolina State University for a postgraduate degree in architecture. "I had always had a strong interest in art, but I couldn't paint and was good at math, so I concentrated this ability on structure and form," notes Foster-Crowder. It turned out that the concept of space was more appealing to her than that of form, and as she struggled along in a class of seventeen students, one of two women, she decided that her ultimate choice would be interiors. "It was, of course, not thought of as serious architecture, and it was what I was expected to do anyway as a woman," she remarks, "but I could see that through developing a knowledge of the use of color, I could create atmosphere. It was a mysterious subject that was not understood or taught at school—like codes, or business, or communication. It was always assumed during the educational experience that a knowledge of design would see you through in the future, an attitude that I found mistaken and appalling. But I have since discovered that some of the most creative people have had similarly uncomfortable feelings while being educated!"

Foster-Crowder made Washington, D.C., her home base in 1979 and worked as a designer at three firms—Swaney Kerns Architects, Interspace Incorporated, and Architectural Interiors, Inc.—before establishing her own business in 1985. "I found out that most firms wanted to be big," she explains, "and this meant doing tenant planning geared to the marketing

Above: The Ceremonial Court exhibit area, in which White House memorabilia is displayed, at the Museum of American History, Smithsonian Institution, Washington, D.C. Photograph by Anice Hoachlander.

effort. I didn't want to do that. I wanted to build to suit individual situations, and do renovations. I wanted to practice excellence in every project that came my way. But I was grateful for what I learned about the really practical aspects of running a business, pragmatic skills of budget management, marketing, and promotion." But she had other philosophical concerns, too—concerns that most large firms cannot address because of their size. These included creating the most attractive working surroundings possible, for maximum productivity and low attrition rate for the client, and environmental awareness. The "green" movement was beginning to gather momentum, and she was eager to learn how the natural resources of earth, air, and water could be husbanded in the process of good design.

Because Foster-Crowder was known to major clients in the D.C. area, including C & P Telephone, Bell Atlantic, and the World Bank, before she set up her own firm, she found that work flowed in the moment she opened her doors. She had established a reputation for good management and good design. C & P Telephone, for example, was particularly pleased with its 750,000-square-foot headquarters, with its paint palette of more than one hundred colors chosen to enhance the architecture of the building while *reducing* interior design costs in terms of wall finishes and dry-wall work stations. Such clients and new ones that followed respected Foster-Crowder for her individuality in resisting current fashions and trends. As she puts it, "I have never taken the safe or predictable road in terms of color. I work with colors that are dateless." As inspirations, Foster-Crowder names traditional Japanese architecture, painter Henri Matisse, the Mexican architect Luis Barragan, and American architect Jon Johansen, who taught for one memorable semester at North Carolina State.

Foster-Crowder takes on no more than ten to twelve projects a year, and they vary from exhibits to showrooms, government and private-sector offices, and museum installations, "geared to keep up a fresh perspective." Recognition for her high standards has come with three IBD awards between 1985 and 1991, in which juries have praised her sense of logic in planning as well as her aesthetic balance.

The United States Chamber of Commerce commissioned her to work on its 1922 Beaux Arts–style building by Cass Gilbert. The task here was to master-plan a conference facility with meeting rooms of various sizes, integrating audio-visual technology, acoustics, lighting, and life-safety design into spaces with stone walls and intricate, inaccessible ceilings. The largest space, the Hall of Flags, posed a serious acoustical problem for both the audience and the television network that often broadcasts from the room. But from a historic perspective, the ceiling, chandeliers, and flags were all sacred and could not be removed. Foster-Crowder started with the floor, using carpet tiles for their sound-absorptive qualities and patterning and replacement capabilities. She created a flaglike motif that aligns with the ceiling grid and echoes its color. The flags were enlarged to obscure the television lights and to accommodate large, rigid, sound-absorptive baffles sandwiched inside them. With this project, she proved her capability with historic renovation and innovation.

However, the 18,000-square-foot headquarters of Public Technology, Incorporated, completed for $25.60 per square foot, demonstrated her energetic creativity in a high-tech manner that was essential to the client, which is on the cutting edge of technological innovation. The company wanted every employee to have an enclosed office, with space and light, without any use of modular furniture. Foster-Crowder planned all the offices to be the same size and placed them on a diagonal in the interior of the space, within the orthogonal building perimeter. Issues of status were solved by creating conference spaces between the offices of senior-level people. By taking an unconventional space-planning approach, to the client's delight, the office promoted both the management and marketing goals of the company.

As leader of a new environmental awareness group in the design community, Foster-Crowder volunteered *pro bono* services to the Friends of the Earth for their new offices in Washington, D.C. The project enabled her to research resources and suppliers, building a useful and ongoing archive of information to share with colleagues in the profession on energy-saving lighting and mechanical devices, nontoxic paints and surface finishes, nonendangered species of wood, recycled materials, and appropriate textiles and furnishings.

Foster-Crowder provides a model case study of how a small firm can survive through excellence and confidence. Her own promotional material, for example, ranks with the best produced by the largest in the profession. It is attractive, consistent, and flexible and spells out its message with brevity and precision, all neatly contained in a lapis-blue booklet that slips into a neat six-by-six-inch white envelope. The package seems to summarize a philosophy that is a message to all: It always pays to do it right.

A selection of Foster-Crowder's work appears on pages 84 to 87.

TRICIA MCCANNON

Dorothy **Harris**

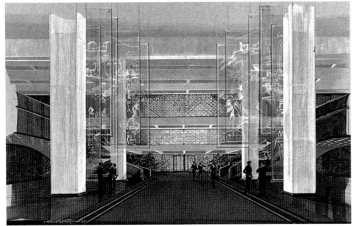

Above: Rendering, lobby with etched-glass panels depicting the history of the Saudi Navy, Royal Saudi Naval Headquarters, Riyadh, Saudi Arabia. Photograph by Ray Elliot.

Every morning when she is not traveling on business, Dorothy Harris rises, puts on jeans, and heads outdoors on her eight-and-a-half-acre farm twenty-three miles from downtown Atlanta to take care of her family: three horses, five goats, one donkey, two dogs, and a cat. Maybe it's nostalgia for a career not taken as a veterinarian. At any rate, Harris realized long ago the importance of de-stressing techniques, in a high-pressure career that has involved overseeing the management and marketing of interior design services for some of the most prestigious blue-chip clients in the country: Ricoh, Bell, Eastman Kodak, Prudential, Wang, Black & Decker, Aetna, and Coca-Cola, not to mention the United States Government's General Services Administration.

Before establishing her own design firm in 1991, Harris was director of interior architecture and design at Rosser Fabrap International, an operation with 450 people on staff. She was one of the first to receive a contract for the 1996 Olympic Games, and completed the offices for the Atlanta Organizing Committee for the Olympic Games in a helter-skelter super-fast-track schedule of fourteen weeks in 1991. But such high-profile clients and hectic deadlines are nothing new for Harris, whose "can do" attitude, professionalism, and sympathetic manner have brought her a constant stream of work for over eighteen years.

Harris graduated from Georgia State University with a bachelor of visual arts in interior design in 1972. Her professor, Richard Stonis, recommended that she interview with three leading Atlanta firms: Heery, Portman, and Associated Space Design (Rosser Fabrap's associate interior-design firm), run by William Pulgram. Pulgram hired her, and the two developed a symbiotic relationship that was to last until he retired almost seventeen years later. Her first project, in an office that was full of young designers in an equal ratio of men to women, was to program an 80,000-square-foot government service office. From there she took on the headquarters of CMI Investment Corporation. But it was when she was four years out of college that she got her major break, on the kind of job that many wait a lifetime to experience, and some never do. This was the new Coca-Cola headquarters in downtown Atlanta.

A battery of talent was lined up to create this prestigious corporate complex, but the then-chairman Paul Austin feared that an overall sense of continuity would be lost. He hired John Chaloner, a New York designer and facilitator working on Coca-Cola's New York offices, to a newly created post of "corporate curator" to orchestrate the personalities and report directly to him. Chaloner, in turn, hired Harris as overall project manager of interiors. "It was my first connection with facility management in a sophisticated way, and I began to understand the real need for a continuity of theme at such a corporate level," says Harris. "It was the difference between a designer looking at one room at a time and a manager who examines the different types of spaces and then tries to coordinate them."

The first year was spent gathering information and working with designers directly on the boards. Subsequently, as a result of their compatible working relationship, Chaloner upgraded Harris to project director. The completion of the 480,000-square-foot Coca-Cola tower in 1980 represented the first phase in an ongoing development of a twenty-three-acre corporate campus. It was also the start of a successful relationship for Harris that still exists today (she has recently completed a project for Coca-Cola Enterprises, the largest bottling company in the United States). To what does she attribute this success? "Most people have no idea what it takes to get a job done," Harris remarks. "Decorators can handle a project of up to 30,000 square feet, but when you start talking about heavy detailing, it has to be managed, built, installed, and documented—and all on time. I have learned that motivating a team to get the job done is as satisfying for me as working on the boards."

In 1975, when the Coca-Cola headquarters project was still in its early stages, the project became the focus of an extremely sensitive conflict between management and shareholders, aggravated by a corporate reluctance to deal with media on "in-house" matters. Highly inflated and inaccurate cost figures appeared in such impeccable sources as the *Wall Street Journal* and *The New York Times*. And it was the interiors, rather than the architecture, that caused the furor. Reports of excessive luxury in the executive offices, the purchase of a museum-quality art collection, and of the involvement of the chairman's wife in selecting furniture, combined with internecine struggles in the corporate hierarchy, kept the story in the news.

Chaloner and Harris embarked on a carefully monitored program that enabled the company to finish up with modest overall costs and thus deflate the exaggerated rumors. The basic building cost was $56 per square foot, compared with the national average of $82 at the time. The total cost of interior furnishings and furniture for all floors was $50 per square foot, compared with the national average of $79 at the time. Much of the cost saving was achieved through the Chaloner/Harris decision to go to open-plan office systems on twenty-one floors and to use one manufacturer, Knoll, for the job. It was the first time a single supplier was used in a mega-building, with the obvious advantages, cost and otherwise, to both vendor and user. The introduction of "corporate standards" was another first in office planning that helped the company consolidate the management

of the building in terms of future procurement and maintenance. Finally, to obtain the neo-Georgian ambience that the executive officers favored, Chaloner went to Korean furniture factories, which offered more competitive pricing than local American suppliers. Again, in the 1970s, this decision was one of the first examples of "off-shore" furniture purchasing, a procedure that was to become commonplace during the office-building boom of the 1980s.

The learning experience was invaluable to Harris, serving as hands-on education in the then-about-to-be-launched discipline of facility management. "I was in the front rank of understanding what this was all about and helped to form the International Facilities Management Association (IFMA) in Atlanta," notes Harris, a debt that the chapter acknowledged in 1990 with the Outstanding Affiliate Member award.

"I never thought that I would be able to top the Coke job, but along came the Army Corps of Engineers, and soon I was working on another first," Harris recalls. "It was the Royal Saudi Naval Headquarters expansion in Riyadh, Saudi Arabia. That was like fairyland or being in the Magic Kingdom." Although Harris never got to attend interviews with the client, because of Saudi protocol concerning contact with women, she nevertheless orchestrated the work on the three-year, $500 million project, which included such details as a $15,000 podium—the one from which General Norman Schwarzkopf was to deliver his press briefings during the 1991 Persian Gulf War.

Asked if she ever feels apprehensive about the final outcome of such mega-projects, Harris responds in the negative and attributes this to her strong background in math and English, which enables her to overcome self-doubt. "I think of every project as having a good beginning and an end, and in the middle is the theme. There is a story no matter what you are working on, but you must start by constructing a scenario that makes sense." She adds, "I also learned that design must be tempered with practicality and related to the priorities that a client places on certain issues, because you must end with a positive, long-lasting impression."

Above: Reception area, Rosser Fabrap International offices, Tampa, Florida. Photograph by George Cott.

A selection of Harris's work appears on pages 88 to 91.

STUART-RODGERS-REILLY

Spes Mekus

Above: Reception area, Coopers & Lybrand offices, Chicago, Illinois. Photograph by Jon Miller, Hedrich-Blessing.

A nalysis is, perhaps, a key element in both architecture and interior design. Before you can come up with a plan, a proposal, or a program for a client, you must analyze the problems that need to be solved. Spes Mekus, partner in Mekus-Johnson, Chicago, has also found it helps to analyze clients, to know more about their personalities, which not only reveals how they think and what their needs might be, but how you can get along with them in the all-important negotiations that are an essential part of the design process. It might seem farfetched to suggest that her first name, which is Latin for "hope," and which was given to her by her father, has been influential in her search for genuineness, yet names and associated words have been seen through the ages as denoting substantive rather than coincidental meaning.

For her guide to personality analysis, Mekus uses Kathy Kolbe's book, *The Conative Connection* (Addison-Wesley, 1990), which presents a new method of measuring creativity, identifying strengths, and predicting human performance on both personal and professional levels. The word *conative* stems from *conation*, the aspect of one's mental activity connected with desire, volition, and striving. It is used in psychology to denote anything connected with the force in one's mental makeup that produces an effort. The Kolbe Concept has been effectively employed to help build teams in many segments of corporate America, including many Fortune 500 companies; to test fighter pilots; and to revitalize sports teams.

Kolbe segments personalities into four broad types: Fact Finder, Quick Start, Follow Thru, and Implementor. Of course, each personality contains a little of all the others, but a given person, according to the statistics recorded by Conative Connection research, is more likely to demonstrate tendencies in one or two of these types. Mekus, predominantly a Quick Start type (catalyst, generalist, innovator, entrepreneur, promoter, improviser), has found the use of this personality-analysis method invaluable in business. "Once a client comes in and we judge what he/she is, we structure our presentations that way, and we now find that it all works out," she explains. "The method has never let us down yet." Convinced by the method's success, Mekus trains her staff to understand how people think and "how to see and have relationships." And, she adds, business has been consistent for her firm, even through tough economic times. She attributes this to having "no single style to our work, and taking into account the personality and culture of each client."

Certainly, there seems to be some special karma working for Mekus, whose office of twenty-five people handles major clients and projects that would more often be the domain of firms three or more times the size. A typical job was the recently completed 650,000-square-foot headquarters of Coopers & Lybrand, one of the "big-eight" accounting firms. Having selected a Skidmore Owings & Merrill building with a glass atrium on the top three floors, the accounting firm turned to Mekus for interior planning and design. She was able to build out a series of undulating "wedding-cake" mezzanines in the three-story atrium that helped increase floor area and create a special focus in the great curving-glass space. This sort of solution—responding to aesthetics and pragmatics—has gained her a successful reputation with international clients, including Budget Rent-A-Car, Citibank, Encyclopedia Britannica, Morton International, Rubloff, and a roster of major law firms.

Mekus emphasizes that she approaches design from the abstract floor plan, as site, sound, rhythm, and light. The process goes far beyond just furnishing and the pragmatics of life-safety for occupants, and derives from her very comprehensive education in the five-year work/study interior design program at the University of Cincinnati (she obtained Bachelor of Arts and Bachelor of Science degrees in 1972), augmented by work at the Harvard Graduate School of Design Continuing Education program in 1981. But it doesn't happen without teamwork. One of her Quick Start qualities, she notes, is her ability to brainstorm (others are accepting challenge and risk, and being able to ad lib, play hunches, experiment, invent, intuit, and promote), which she makes a point of doing in the design studio. "I like to motivate and help generate ideas, build and develop other people," she says.

Motivation as the driving force was a key asset when Mekus established the Illinois Interior Design Coalition (IIDC) as founding president in the mid-1980s. The objective was licensing for interior designers, a sensitive issue in a state and a city (home to Frank Lloyd Wright, Ludwig Mies van der Rohe, and Louis Sullivan) known for its supremacy in architecture. There was great resistance to the IIDC title licensing bill, from both architects and designers, with behind-the-scenes sabotage and intensive lobbying by people who were misguided and un-

Above: Office interiors for Mekus-Johnson Inc, Chicago. Photograph by Jon Miller, Hedrich-Blessing.

informed, or just plain terrified of the consequences. Mekus was unfazed and pursued the objective, acquiring the necessary funding, and gathering the spiritual momentum from designers, to see the bill become enacted in 1990. Quick Starts, according to Kathy Kolbe, are known for trying things another way and pride themselves on doing the undoable. Mekus was not going to give up on this goal. "I had experienced chauvinistic prejudice many times: in school, when my professor said that if I wanted a career in decorating—which I did not but he supposed I did—I was in the wrong place. At a men's club in Chicago with a special entrance for women, I refused to be segregated in this instance and walked in the same entrance. I found out nothing could be done about it. Being a rebel worked."

People who know Mekus are equally impressed with her businesslike attitude, which she affirms is vital for anyone in an entrepreneurial position, running his or her own firm: "Working for large architectural firms as a coop student, I quickly got to understand that selling ideas was important, being logical and articulate was the point. You had to get people to buy into your propositions." If she has a mentor to thank for her will to pursue her goals with utmost determination, it would be, she says, her father: "He laid down the precept that life is a continual process of learning and making the most of yourself." Thus, she explains, "I put my career first and thought everything else would follow, which it did, including marriage and family. I have still found time to bring up two human beings, be a nurturer, *and* stand on a soapbox."

Stepping down from the presidency of IIDC after three years of active effort, Mekus has turned her attention more recently to the Chicago Interior Design Organization, an ad hoc group that meets to further cooperation, rather than dog-eat-dog competition, among the city's many interior design firms. Says Mekus, "We all share the same objective—to educate the client base into understanding the value of what we do and the services we provide. If we all work together, the synthesis will provide more for everyone in the future." To achieve this goal, Mekus will probably focus on the Quick Start modes, which prevent stress and accommodate needs. They include acting fluently, intuitively, insightfully, spontaneously, adventurously, imaginatively, conceptually and, if necessary, defiantly.

A selection of Mekus's work appears on pages 92 to 95.

PACH BROTHERS

Julia **Monk**

Probably the most significant commitment to architectural restoration in the United States in the 1990s is the rehabilitation of four major hotels from the turn of the century—a program implemented by ITT Sheraton at a cost of more than $500 million. Of the four—the Moana Surfrider in Honolulu, Hawaii, the Jefferson in Richmond, Virginia, the Palace in San Francisco, and the St. Regis in New York City— the latter is the crown jewel. It was finished in the fall of 1991, at a time when the economy seemed uncertain. Yet well before the doors opened, the management was receiving requests for rooms from clients who had stayed at the hotel for decades and who were more than willing to pay the increased price of $400-plus per night for a double room, and as much as $2,700 per night for a suite.

The renovation of the St. Regis Hotel, under the direction of Julia Monk, president of Brennan Beer Gorman Monk/Interiors, New York, was quite simply the talk of the town, representing an authentic replication of the original hotel, built for John Jacob Astor in 1904, with an addition in 1927. Original marble floors were revealed in the foyer and corridors, original paneling refurbished and augmented, and original ceilings re-exposed and gold-leafed, with discreetly located new mechanical installations for the heating and air-conditioning systems.

Furthermore, four new rooms were created for private functions—the Tiffany, the Dior, the Presidential, and the St. Regis—and the King Cole Bar, a legendary rendezvous for decades, was refurbished, once again decorated with its famous Maxfield Parrish "King Cole" mural.

For Monk, the $100-million project was a coup, but it was only one of many in a brief career highlighted with outstanding successes. Graduating from Ball State University in Muncie, Indiana, in 1978, with a five-year degree in architecture and environmental design, Monk was singled out as one of the most promising students (one of 6 women in a class of 120), receiving the Alpha Rho Chi and AIA scholastic achievement awards. She headed for Chicago, her hometown, and joined Perkins & Will as a design draftsperson. "They were in the middle of a design competition, and I worked straight for two and a half days to see it completed," she recalls. "So I stepped right up to bat."

Above: Corporate offices, New York City. Photograph by Peter Paige.

When a colleague rejected an assignment working on the Juffali Headquarters Office Building in Jidda, Saudi Arabia, Monk accepted it and learned the power of positivism. As she puts it, "I have never said 'no' to anything, and I think that has helped me in moving forward in my career." The Jidda job involved working with a sheik in a country prejudiced against giving women responsibility. Yet she succeeded in winning influence and even made three trips to Saudi Arabia, with Sheik Juffali taking responsibility for her stay and listening to her advice on each occasion. "It was a soup-to-nuts job," Monk remarks. "I found out that the sheik's wife had a significant role, so I was able to develop a friendship with her that helped the project along."

In the downturn of the economy in the early 1980s, Monk was transferred to the New York office of Perkins & Will, promoted to senior project designer, and worked on a slew of big jobs: the Newport City Master Plan in Jersey City, New Jersey; the Perimeter Center West, Atlanta, Georgia; the Lever Brothers offices in Englewood Cliffs, New Jersey; the Bank of New York in Wilmington, Delaware; Integon corporate headquarters in Winston-Salem, North Carolina; and Crown Pointe in Atlanta. She never experienced any problems as a woman architect while involved in such projects and believes that she was in the happy position of following the early militants, who paved the way for other women professionals to follow. "I have never been active in the women's movement as a women's libber, partly because I have worked with men who were always supportive," she claims. "I don't feel I have ever been under-recognized in my work. I find the worst attitude toward businesswomen is likely to be in the first or business class sections on airplanes, where men seem to be much better treated by the flight attendants than women."

In 1984, when Henry Brennan, Peter Gorman, and David Beer decided to leave Perkins & Will, they asked Monk to join them as their first employee. After consulting with her father, an engineer, she agreed to take the risk, provided that they move out of an apartment-based office and get proper office space. They did and she joined the firm.

By 1986 the office had expanded to seventy people and Monk was named the firm's first associate, having worked on several key jobs in Hartford, Connecticut, designing hotels such as the Essex House, the Sherry-Netherland, and the Sutton in New York, and two restaurants in Washington, D.C., as well as having supervised the immense Sheraton Centre Hotel renovation proposal in New York City. It was on the latter project that she encountered her first gender-related opposition from a client. Her partners supported her, however, and she proved she could do the job. When the clients returned with a plum job, the St. Regis, they requested that Monk be in charge.

Monk credits two professors—Dan Woodfin and Kunud Friis, a visiting critic from Denmark at Ball State—with giving her the well-rounded education that now enables her to solve clients' problems: "At a time when design was considered 100 percent of the issue, they told me that it was only really 75 per-

Above: Gallery Urban, New York City. Photograph by Peter Paige.

cent of the issue and that at least 25 percent of the effort had to go into solving problems. Too often, architects throw a bunch of clichés together that look as if they solve the problem, but in fact they don't get to the essence of the matter." She concentrates on making clear statements in circulation paths and letting forms follow plan rather than the other way around.

A year after being made associate, Monk made another leap forward. By this time the firm had expanded to ninety people, twenty under her direct supervision in the interiors division, and the founding partners decided to make her the firm's first new partner. They offered her a three percent stake in the architectural partnership or a 100 percent stake as president of a new interiors firm. "I wrestled with that decision for six weeks," she laughs. "It was a hard one to make, but finally I went for the status of president, with the gut feeling that interiors were going to get stronger in terms of business in the future." Only twelve years into her career, Monk has demonstrated an excellence that has taken her to the top of her profession. While she is the first to admit that she has been exposed to extraordinary circumstances, she also points out, rather shyly, that personal ability has a lot to do with it: "I know I am good at what I do."

A selection of Monk's work appears on pages 96 to 99.

RUVEN ASANADOR

Rita **St. Clair**

Above: Dining area, private residence, San Francisco, California.

When Rita St. Clair was named national president of the American Society of Interior Designers (ASID) in 1979, many observers saw the decision as a turning point in the organization's history. Up until then, ASID was widely perceived as being composed of "decorators" and "ladies with hats." St. Clair's election was proof that the Society had become something more. Interior designers were no longer just residentially oriented but were in charge of major corporate and commercial work, at home and abroad. A designer running her own business in Baltimore, Maryland, since 1968, St. Clair boasted a client list that spoke to this change. It was about 70 percent commercial (offices, hotels, and restaurants) and 30 percent residential.

St. Clair's vigorous stewardship of the Society during her tenure in office forecasted the gathering momentum and influence of interior designers as they branched out into auxiliary services through the decade of the 1980s: space planning, lease negotiation, facility management, and allied work that went far beyond the selection of fabrics and furnishings, resulting in what St. Clair calls "the cannibalization of architecture." She also focused members' attention on the broad-based needs of the public—needs such as affordable housing, pleasant surroundings in public-transportation facilities, and environments accessible to people with disabilities. It has been more than a decade since she first perceived these needs, and as a prophet she feels she is still in the wilderness: "We keep forgetting that our original mandate is to serve and educate the public. Only when you do this can you have a healthy economic base for the profession. The perpetuation of the organization and the profession is secondary to the health of the public." However, her farsightedness helped the Society grow to its current membership of 30,000 and move its headquarters from New York City to Washington, D.C., where it is in closer contact with government legislation affecting the profession.

For more than twenty-four years, St. Clair has been operating out of the same gracious nineteenth-century townhouse in Baltimore. Much of the original character of the building has been retained, but space has been appropriately allocated for her twenty-person staff, which includes twelve designers. Accounting and clerical activities are carried out on the lower level, reception and conferencing areas are on the ground floor,

Above left: The Diana chair, designed by St. Clair, is manufactured and sold by David Edward Limited.

Above right: The Alexandra, a custom chair design by St. Clair.

and studios and her own office are located upstairs. The ambience is one of decorative richness, suggesting a cosmopolitan attitude—St. Clair has a satellite office in Florence, Italy, where she spends every summer, and she also travels considerably. Along the way, she is likely to buy furniture and objects, sometimes with a specific job in mind, sometimes to inventory for future clients. Wall hangings from Indonesia, screens, fans, ceramics, silver, paintings, and antiques from Europe and the Far East are arranged in inviting vignettes in what was originally the lofty-ceilinged front parlor of the house. Her predilection for purchases recently led her to buy the adjacent townhouse, which she now operates as a retail shop called Findings, a "warehouse of treasures to sell with our work, or to the public direct."

Upon leaving the University of Iowa with a bachelor of fine arts degree, St. Clair wanted to work in the art world, to be involved with contemporary painting in some way, but she needed a job and landed one at a Baltimore dealership selling Knoll and Herman Miller furniture. In that job she learned to appreciate modern furniture and signed up at Parsons School of Design for further education.

When she became pregnant in 1957, and her employer decided it was "time to stop working," she launched her own business. "Clients started calling me for advice on color and lighting," she recalls, "so I started working out of my kitchen at home. I opened my first office in 1964 with two people. I still have the same accountants and attorneys that I had then." Although she began with a preference for a modern vocabulary, St. Clair learned to develop her portfolio of services for clients, with an understanding that their requirements came first. She found she enjoyed traditional interiors and was delighted to be chosen for the renovation of Baltimore's nineteenth-century city hall in 1976 and the refurbishing of the city's Center Stage Theatre. Both projects received citations. From the early days, she started winning awards, for both interior and product de-

signs, a result that she attributes to her personal supervision on crucial aspects of a project: "I will always insist on being on a job when paints are tried out. Things like that make a difference. You can't afford to let the client in for repainting expenses, when the work doesn't come out the way you intended."

Her hotel work, in particular—including the Belvedere Hotel, Baltimore, the Netherland Plaza Hotel, Cincinnati, and the Peabody Court Hotel, Baltimore—has won her recognition. The common denominator in these projects is an atmosphere of grandeur and luxury, related to the architecture of the building. In the Netherland Plaza, for example, an art deco restoration, St. Clair went to painstaking efforts to identify plasterwork, metal artistry, rosewood panels, painted murals, and architectural detailing buried under travesties of 1950s' modern refurbishments, and insisted that these be put on the priority list for revival. However, at the Intercontinental Hotel in Miami her theme was "tropical contemporary," which she expertly realized with trelliswork, pastels, and custom carpeting with an abstract design of lagoons and palm trees. In recognition of these and many other achievements, St. Clair was inducted into *Interior Design* magazine's Hall of Fame in 1989.

St. Clair finds the challenge of hospitality work particularly stimulating, because it goes far beyond the aesthetic level to deeper problem solving. "A restaurant can look magnificent, but if it isn't sympathetic to the needs of the chef in the kitchen and the waiters serving customers, and if the clients don't have comfortable seats and lighting they can read the menu by, then it will simply go out of business very fast," she says over lunch at Baltimore's Polo Grill at the Inn at the Colonnade, one of her recent jobs. This restaurant has become a favorite Baltimore haunt and resonates with the conservative nature of the city, its dark green painted paneling, leather seating, and subdued lighting creating the aura of an exclusive club. She continues, "Restaurant design is also an area that must respond to changing life-styles. Hospitality work is about two things—creating fantasy and the bottom line." She adds, "It's essentially temporary because it's programmed for a redo in five to seven years, or even earlier. Life-cycle costs are built in at the start."

These days, St. Clair's success in the hospitality market has resulted in inquiries from Japan, and she includes a sheet in Japanese in her firm's brochure. And just as she is aware of the need to develop overseas markets, she recognizes the important shifts in the profession: "I would not have thought when I was ASID president that I would ever say that interior design education is inadequate, but today I believe that it is." She recommends that anyone interested in interior design enroll in architecture school for the required four years, then spend two more years studying interior design and two more in the field, before launching out to practice. "It's still less time than it takes a physician to qualify," she points out, "and both are concerned with the public's health and well-being."

A selection of St. Clair's work appears on pages 100 to 103.

BRIAN SMITH

Lynn Wilson

Above: Restaurant, Biltmore Hotel, Coral Gables, Florida.
Photograph by Carl Francetic.

A black, two-seater Jaguar slides into its parking place on Majorca Avenue in Coral Gables, Florida, and out steps designer Lynn Wilson, business-suited in slick anthracite gray and white pinstripes, armed with a fat legal briefcase in one hand and a large glass vase of flowers in the other. She heard that the office cleaner broke the vase on her black lacquer desk while she was away on a business trip, and flowers, she insists, are an important psychological lift during a twelve-hour working day. Wilson is generally first in and last out of the office—when at the home base. This week's itinerary has been typical: Miami to London to Paris to Tokyo, where she wound up visiting a Japanese client who has retained her to work on a multimillion-dollar golf resort, which includes 236-plus hotel rooms, 200 condominiums, 13 restaurants, and a gymnasium-swim club. Today is Friday and she will review plans and projects in progress during her absence. She climbs the elephant-gray carpeted stairs to her office, where a businesslike gray-and-white theme, with modern steel-and-lacquer furniture sets a tone that reflects her streamlined, modern approach to design.

Now in the top-ten list of the nation's hospitality designers, with a 350-person firm in five cities (Miami, London, Paris, Los Angeles, and Ventnor, New Jersey), Wilson started her firm working out of the den of her first home, at age twenty-seven, when she had three children under six years of age to care for. She has used her ad hoc entrepreneurial talents to build a portfolio of work over the past twenty years, though she claims that this was really not her goal when she set out.

However, with a mother who had been a Martha Graham company dancer and a Radio City Rockette, and a father who was a composer and musician, Wilson was clearly destined for an artistic career. After graduating (as a scholarship student) from the University of Miami, with a master's degree in art history and a bachelor's degree in advertising and design, with a minor in architecture ("I was hungry for education and packed it all in."), she first joined I.D. Associates, a Miami, Florida, firm that specialized in "total" design. "Everything was a unified concept," Wilson explains, "right down to graphics, menus, and uniforms, if we were doing a hotel or restaurant. It was very good training for me, because I learned about consistency. I saw the wisdom of this system and later the advantage to clients. Too often a developer will contract many consultants all over the place, but to have a truly successful result, a project will benefit from consistency with one overall consultant." (Wilson now makes a point of hiring specialists in all aspects of the job, so that her firm can offer multiple services under one roof.)

When the partners had a tiff about eighteen months after she started in the firm, she was told she was "overqualified" and was laid off. She was working on two hotels and a 600-seat restaurant at the time and had begun to build a client base of her own. Within six months of working out of her home, word-of-mouth recommendations made it possible for her to open up her own office with a secretary, a draftsman, and an assistant designer. "Perhaps I was fortunate then, but I have never advertised or done any marketing," says Wilson. "I have succeeded by people hearing about my work. It perpetuates itself."

Wilson's roster of projects includes eighty-seven well-known resorts and hotels, from Caesar's Palace in Las Vegas to the Harley Hotel in New York City, from the Biltmore in Coral Gables to the Rittenhouse in Philadelphia, and numerous seaside destinations in between. The world's hoteliers—Sheraton, Marriott, Holiday Inn, Disney, and Hyatt—have called on her unique range of services, which begins with theme and concept creation and encompasses all the nitty-gritty considerations (budget analysis, contract documents, specifications, bidding, and purchasing) as well as the "glamour" aspects of the interior design and architecture, including the purchasing of museum-quality works of art.

Once a job is landed, Wilson designates a studio team with a job captain to see it through and kicks off with a half-day brainstorming session, during which she briefs the team on the client's ideas and gathers her initial thoughts and concepts about the project. What is typical of Wilson's work is that nothing is typical. Unlike many of her competitors in the hospitality-design field, she does not offer a "look." She prefers to derive inspiration for a concept by considering the geography, culture, and location of the site, along with the corporate culture and personality of the client. Each hotel is thus distinctive and different. The Ship's Bar at the Rittenhouse Hotel, for example, displays models of antique sailing ships to define the history of Philadelphia as a maritime port; wild ducks indigenous to the Florida marshlands were chosen for wallpaper and motifs in the Ocala Hilton Hotel dining room; and a rigorously researched restoration of the 1930s' Coral Gables Biltmore Hotel—down to gold leafing and craftsman-executed mill work—re-creates the feeling of an authentic Spanish *palacio*.

Wilson herself will ensure this distinction, even if it takes her up a muddy jungle river in Indonesia in search of primitive baskets and accessories, which it has. She thrives on

Above: Mary Cassatt Tea Garden, Rittenhouse Hotel, Philadelphia. Photograph by Tom Crane.

projects that exploit her love of archaeology, such as the new Mediterranean village-theme hotel at Disney World, which she worked on with architect Antoine Predock. Her ideas here included the Petra Bar, a fantasy in *faux* stone recalling an ancient city site in Jordan. Listening to clients is one way, she insists, to ensure quality and distinction. For example, when working on the Ocala Hilton with developer Ed Gadinsky, she helped develop a new concept for the Honeymoon Suite: "Ed and his wife wanted to use the hotel as their home-away-from-home from time to time. They liked the idea of an oversize bathroom, with lots of natural light, that allowed them to use it together." The design included the latest whirlpool-equipped tub, two washbasins, a walk-in shower, and dressing and exercise areas. It was a "first" of its kind, as it took up just as much space as a normal hotel bathroom and bedroom usually occupy!

With her reputation for high-quality, on-time, and on-budget performances, along with her sizable annual revenues, Wilson has attracted media attention, which in turn has led to her being the first woman executive in the Southeast region invited to join the Young Presidents Organization. It was not long after accepting membership that Wilson was contacted by the Harvard Business School to participate in a Case Study Program. She was asked to explain her methodology which, as she puts it, is "totally different from anything that is accepted procedure." For example, she hires strong people who are competent at all levels, not just skilled at the top of the pyramid, and she has always rejected short-term thinking in favor of long-term planning and the needs of the client. "I have developed business instincts on the job, unpolluted by academic business philosophies, but it seems to have worked. I have never once not made payroll."

Dealing with the unconventional, however, has been Wilson's career story. As she observes, right from the beginning she has been out on a limb: the only female in the University of Miami Architecture School, as well as its only cheerleader, with a determination not to wind up "doing the garden-club thing" but to work in a "man's field." At the end of the day in Coral Gables, she drives back to her serene waterfront villa in Miami Beach, and enjoys the fruits of her success. It is a home of great quality and style, decorated elegantly in an assemblage of paintings, antique furnishings, and objects from many parts of the world, each chosen for its artistic merit, and augmented with grand bouquets of flowers in every room. She is particularly drawn to eighteenth-century European antiques and Pre-Columbian ceramics. But even on her own turf, she is more likely to be thinking about business and figuring out her next move: "how to be truly global."

A selection of Wilson's work appears on pages 104 to 107.

JIM ALLEN

Trisha **Wilson**

Above: Lobby lounge, Waterfront Centre Hotel, Vancouver, British Columbia. Photograph by Mary Nichols.

I n a presentation meeting to the Walt Disney Company, the Trisha Wilson & Associates team from Dallas, Texas, did a show-business number that they felt was appropriate for the occasion. They dressed in Western-style clothes—boots, belts, denims, and hats—and carried lassoes, much to the astonishment of their competitors interviewing for Disney projects with them. The strategy turned out to be a typical success story in the history of Wilson's career. Her firm not only got the job they hoped to get, but Michael Eisner, Disney's chairman and CEO, was so taken by their act that they walked out with *three* major projects for EuroDisneyland. And they were plum jobs: the interiors of hotels by internationally celebrated architects Robert A. M. Stern, Anton Grumbach, and Antoine Predock, recently opened in the new Disney fantasyland outside Paris.

Theatrical pizzazz has served Wilson well, right from the start when, as an interior design graduate from the University of Texas, Austin, she took her first job in 1969 at Titche-Goettinger, a Dallas department store, in the furniture department. It was a sales job, and she worked on the usual commission-only basis. "That was how I learned to sell; it was invaluable," she says. Upon taking over the interior design department at the store, she learned how to solve problems, and when a customer said he was opening a restaurant and asked her to do the job on a freelance basis, she got her first break. Wilson explains: "It was 1971. Dallas was changing and approving [the serving of] liquor by the drink. I suddenly became known as 'the restaurant designer.' And that's how it all snowballed."

She left the store to open her own firm, working out of her apartment with an assistant. When Dallas developer Trammel Crow announced a plan to build the Anatole Hotel, opposite his World Trade Center located outside downtown Dallas, she was determined to get the job. By the time the interview was set up, she had identified four people she wanted on her team if she were to get the assignment. Her enthusiasm impressed Crow: she won the commission and was soon creating the first of a new kind of Texas hotel, a 600-room complex with six restaurants, an art-filled atrium, and a conference center accessed by escalators, later to be extended by several hundred more rooms, another atrium, a health club, and some private suites decorated with palatial silk and velvet—"Dynasty"-style sumptuousness that became an integral aspect of the Wilson design signature.

As the Anatole job was winding down in 1979, Wilson worked out her next marketing strategy. The office with six staff just didn't look prosperous enough to attract a major project from Sheraton. She rented the space next door, pulled down some walls, moved in some rental furniture, and asked half a dozen friends to sit at the desks when the client arrived on the premises. "I was so naïve that I just didn't know that I couldn't make it," Wilson remarks. "My head told me to go for it." She got it. And from this small beginning her hospitality-design firm has mushroomed to include offices in New York, Los Angeles, London, and Singapore, with a total of 135 people on the payroll. Marketing tactics to bring in new clients have escalated to include such extravagances as renting a motor yacht, hiring three bands and the best caterers in New York City, and cruising around Manhattan for an evening with two hundred guests dressed in evening clothes.

"I have always felt hospitality was right for me," remarks Wilson, who enjoys giving parties and playing hostess, "and a job generally includes all aspects of design: the rooms are like residential design, the conference spaces and administration offices are like corporate design, the lobbies are public spaces, and health clubs, restaurants, and discos are the leisure design. There's a lot of human interaction and I find it more fun than corporate office work," she adds. "The best part about it is that unlike corporate work, the general public gets to see your efforts."

Over the past decade, the Wilson approach has evolved from an interior decorator approach, with an emphasis on finishes, fixtures, paint chips and fabrics, to a far more sophisticated architectural capability. The ratio of architects to interior designers on the Wilson staff has changed dramatically to the present balance of 70 percent architects to 30 percent interior designers. This came about in response to the need for more detailed drawings and three-dimensional models, combined with the necessity of conducting close relationships with base-building architects, engineers, special consultants, and construction managers. She finds architects more qualified to do this work, and while they may not have the experience required in choosing finishing materials, they are flexible enough to learn. Conversely, she declares, it is much harder to teach an interior designer the finer points of architecture if the discipline hasn't been part of her educational process.

Like many Texans, Wilson has been driven to explore markets overseas to keep her firm buoyant, and while travel is high on her agenda, with as much as 90 percent of the work coming from abroad, she does not "market" full time at the expense of designing. "I still try to make 60 percent of my time billable to a job," she says, "and I assign special projects to myself because I feel it's important to keep my hand in." And despite the number of jobs—up to forty-plus—going through at one time, she has a system that enables her to keep track of them all. Every Friday, project managers present their status reports, so that by reading them over the weekend, she can answer any questions the clients might pitch directly to her.

She takes a very personal, hands-on approach with staff as well, many of whom have been with her for more than ten years, including her secretary. "Any business is people," she comments. "I never had any management training, but I make sure that office morale is high and spirits are up. People's attitudes and personalities must be carefully considered at all times." A lack of strict-bottom-line accounting allows her to keep her staff happy by paying for babysitters when single working mothers are sent off abroad on a job, and even paying for dog- and cat-sitters if necessary. In-house parties are a customary happening and may include lavish dinners for 60 in a Dallas restaurant when the home-base staff celebrates Wilson's birthday. Employee anniversaries may be marked with gifts of custom-ordered jewelry. But like all entrepreneurial leaders, she has found such small friendly favors more often than not are offset by productivity generated through employee satisfaction, which eventually reflects beneficially on revenues.

The *esprit de corps* and joy of working is evident throughout the Dallas offices where the firm is headquartered, and where currently work is finishing up on the most lavish project ever executed by the Wilson team, the Palace Hotel in the Lost City, a new resort for safari vacationers in Bophuthatswana, South Africa. A budget of 2 million rand was allocated for this hotel, which is in close proximity to the safari territories little known to tourists as yet. Details include crystal-and-bronze stair railings, mega-scale public areas, safari-themed suites with animal-print fabrics, and custom-made furniture, including four-poster beds, in each of the 350 rooms. It is a once-in-a-lifetime job that Wilson herself directed.

Asked about planning by objective, Wilson says she has never made a five-year plan, for fear that she would complete it in less than that time. She prefers to move "from A to B, rather than A to Z." A driving force keeps her rolling and is appreciated by her Texan peers, who make certain her energy is channeled to numerous causes: the University of Texas at Austin, Texas Historical Records, the Texas State Fair, the Texas Business Hall of Fame Foundation, the Dallas Assembly, and the Young President's Organization, to name just a few. Whatever comes her way, her attitude is definitely positive. And her fail-safe directive—optimism—is reflected in the very fine black-leather bibelot on her desk, with its crisp message tooled in gold leaf, facing out toward visitors: *It can be done.*

A selection of Wilson's work appears on pages 108 to 111.

Above and left: A small, 3,000-square-foot space for National Westminster Bank, in a Fox & Fowle–designed building in midtown Manhattan, offered high ceilings, which allowed a mezzanine to be inserted, creating sufficient space for tellers at street level and support staff above. The two levels are linked by an elegant, coiling stairway. The teller counter echoes the shape of a mezzanine wall and is topped with a ribbon of protective glass. Photograph by Peter Paige.

Opposite: A major renovation transformed a ten-floor structure (once the flagship Ohrbachs department store), on Manhattan's West 34th Street, into a mixed-use office building. At street level, a new double-height vaulted entrance vestibule and lobby were created. The interior finishes, including granite, marble, brass, and bronze, respond to the building's stately granite and limestone façade. Photograph by Fred George.

Left, top and bottom: Located near Times Square, the 460-room Embassy Suites Hotel offers thirty-eight floors of hotel, public, and retail spaces. The interiors are expressive of the building's context—at the heart of the Broadway Theater District and the entertainment center of New York City. Spotlights attached to horizontal and vertical grid structures are reminiscent of theatrical lighting systems. Burns's use of bright primary colors adds a sense of vitality to the spaces. Photographs by Peter Paige.

Above: The pattern of the marble tile floor in the lobby of the Embassy Suites Hotel in New York City intentionally—and artfully— recalls Piet Mondrian's abstract painting Broadway Boogie Woogie. *Photograph by Peter Paige.*

Above: For the corporate headquarters of the Hechinger Company in Washington, D.C., Foster-Crowder designed a double-height reception area to display selections from the firm's impressive art collection. Transparent glass walls were installed, allowing the movement of employees in this 237,000-square-foot facility to enliven the space. Photograph by Jeff Heger.

Opposite: In the three-story main lobby space of the C & P Telephone Company headquarters in Silver Spring, Maryland, Foster-Crowder used color to add a human touch to what could have been a rather cold, imposing space. Over 100 colors were selected to orchestrate a palette of warmth and welcome to the 120,000-square-foot facility. Photograph by Tom Crane.

Above: The Hall of Flags at the United States Chamber of Commerce in Washington, D.C., is used as a reception/conference room. Large flags, displayed along the sides of the room, obscure unsightly television lighting panels and accommodate sound-absorbing baffles sandwiched inside them. The carpeting was designed by Foster-Crowder to respond to the grid pattern and colors of the intricately painted ceiling. Photograph by Anice Hoachlander.

Left: The Ceremonial Court at the Smithsonian Institution's Museum of American History is where White House memorabilia from the National Collection is displayed. Working with White House historians and Smithsonian curators, Foster-Crowder designed a suite of rooms that are intended to capture the character of the mansion during Theodore Roosevelt's tenure as President. Many pieces that originally furnished the White House, including the torchères at left, have been incorporated into the design scheme. Photograph by Anice Hoachlander.

Opposite: The Clare Booth Luce conference room, at the School of Foreign Service building on the campus of Georgetown University in Washington, D.C., is furnished with pieces offering the curvilinearity that would have been popular during the height of this influential American businesswoman and ambassador's life. The colors were selected to harmonize with those of a portrait of Mrs. Luce that is the focus of the space. Photograph by Anice Hoachlander.

Above: Classic Barcelona chairs hug the walls in the handsomely rendered circular reception area of the offices of the Atlanta Committee for the Olympic Games. Photograph by Rion C. Rizzo.

Left: A gallery, hung with posters advertising Olympic Games of the past, leads from the reception area to a freestanding circular presentation/briefing room at the Atlanta Committee for the Olympic Games headquarters. Photograph by Rion C. Rizzo.

Above: The curved reception seating area on the executive floor of the Coca-Cola Enterprises building in Atlanta, Georgia, is backed by built-in display windows, with soft-drink bottles and cans, drinking glasses, packaging designs, and other company memorabilia on view. The gridded lacquered wood wall creates a motif that is applied throughout the offices on the floor. Photograph by Rion C. Rizzo.

Left: The boardroom at Coca-Cola Enterprises is nestled within the executive floor. A custom-designed table and credenza are the high-lights of the space, which is hand-somely lit using direct and indirect methods. The room's illumination

and audio-visual equipment can be manually operated or pre-programmed at the podium. Photograph by Rion C. Rizzo.

Opposite: To celebrate the commu-nity surrounding the company's offices at The Atlantic Center in Atlanta, Georgia, IBM commis-sioned renowned photographer Joel Meyerowitz to record features of this urban landscape. For the photogra-phy exhibition, Harris installed a display system similar to construc-tion scaffolding, selecting hanging and framing materials straight from a hardware store—reinforc-ing the urban theme of the show. Photograph by Rion C. Rizzo.

Above: For the Santa Fe Southern Pacific Corporation, a giant $13 billion conglomerate, a newly renovated landmark building in Chicago was utilized as the firm's 224,000-square-foot headquarters. Immaculately appointed secretarial stations were given a luxurious detail: a round window with a spectacular view of Lake Michigan. Photograph by Jim Hedrich, Hedrich-Blessing.

*Above: A restricted design budget
for SPSS Inc., a software development company, dictated high-tech
space planning. A custom-designed
serpentine reception desk incorporates a glass shelf affixed with colorful hardware. Photograph by Jon
Miller, Hedrich-Blessing.*

*Overleaf: East meets Midwest in the
offices of Masuda, Funai, Eifert &
Mitchell, a Japanese-American law
firm in Chicago, Illinois. The firm's
13,500-square-foot headquarters
responds to the Japanese culture's
fondness for simplicity and serenity.
In the reception area, post-and-
beam bench seating was installed
along one wall. Wooden blinds
shade a standard fluorescent light
fixture, creating a natural skylight
effect. The shoji-like door slides
open to admit visitors to the inner
offices. Photograph by Jon Miller,
Hedrich-Blessing.*

Above: Sumptuous marble balustrades, columns, and tile flooring, crystal chandeliers, and elaborate ironwork give the Astor Court at New York City's St. Regis Hotel the ambience of a palace. Photograph by Oberto Gili.

Left: The front desk of the St. Regis has been faithfully restored. The lobby's original half-vaulted ceiling was uncovered, as was the intricately patterned marble floor, a 1904 gem which had been hidden under wall-to-wall carpeting. Photograph by Anthony P. Albarello.

Opposite: ITT Sheraton spent over $100 million on the renovation of the St. Regis Hotel on Manhattan's Fifth Avenue. The work included the complete gutting of the guest-room floors and the refurbishing and refinishing of the baroque-style 1904 public spaces on the entrance lobby floor. As part of the lavish interior program, a new off-the-lobby atrium space called the Astor Court was created. Its lofty ceiling is enhanced with trompe l'oeil clouds and sky and painted panels depicting mythological scenes. Photograph by Oberto Gili.

Above: This ornate reception room at the St. Regis combines elements of the Louis XV and XVI styles, with lavish gilded mirrors, regally swagged draperies, elaborate chandeliers and sconces, and rich boiserie. Photograph by Oberto Gili.

Right: The original wood paneling and marble fireplace were restored in the Louis XVI Room at the St. Regis. The carpet, a custom design, covers new wood flooring. Photograph by Anthony P. Albarello.

Opposite: The richly colored and decorated Cognac Room of the St. Regis serves as an intimate conversation area off the lobby. An ornate chandelier and marble-topped gilded Boulle cabinet were original pieces found in the hotel. The cornices are detailed in twenty-two karat gold leaf. Photograph by Oberto Gili.

Top: Opened in 1931, the Netherland Plaza Hotel in Cincinnati,
Ohio, was a splendidly ornate
establishment executed in the
popular art deco style. Recently
landmarked, the hotel underwent
as authentic a restoration as possible, as the interiors had undergone
several "modernization" programs
since the 1950s. Its Hall of Mirrors
is a glittering space with a trompe
l'oeil painted ceiling and an elabo-
rately detailed balcony railing.
Photograph by Norman McGrath.

Above: A cocktail bar in the Palm
Court of the Netherland Plaza
Hotel was deftly designed to fit into
the art deco context. Its polished
bronze, steel, and glass canopy

creatively incorporates lighting and
glass-storage racks. Photograph by
Norman McGrath.

Left: In the hotel's Palm Court
restaurant, St. Clair restored original rosewood paneling and historic
murals, and installed new lighting
to highlight decorative details.
Photograph by Norman McGrath.

Left: The decorative theme of the Palm Court restaurant at the Hotel Intercontinental, Miami, Florida, is based on trelliswork and a series of updated garden gazebo spaces. Photograph by Dan Forer.

Below left: The atrium lobby of the Miami Intercontinental projects a tropical Florida atmosphere. Wicker porch chairs and banquettes are arranged on colorful carpets adorned with collages of flamingo-pink islands and exotic green foliage. Photograph by Dan Forer.

Above: A private office suite for the chairman of the board of U.S. Fidelity and Guaranty, Baltimore, Maryland, was designed by St. Clair to express the personality and taste of its occupant. Fine pieces of Asian art and an eclectic mix of traditional and contemporary furnishings contribute to the deliberately residential, non-office-like business setting. Photograph by Paul Warchol.

Right: The lobby at Baltimore's Inn at the Colonnade was interpreted in a classical style. Satinwood panels the walls and veneers the columns, whose capitals are decorated with Egyptian motifs. The domed ceiling was painted with a skyscape. St. Clair designed the octagonally shaped rug especially for the room.

Left, top and bottom: Wilson's own residence in Miami Beach, Florida, is a Spanish-style courtyard house, built in 1930 for the Hoover (vacuum cleaner) family. Though impressive, it offers a sense of relaxed formality that is appropriate to its location. It is also a personal gallery of sorts, filled with antiques, artworks, and artifacts collected by the designer on her travels throughout the world. The seventeenth-century chandelier in the living room was originally wired for the Hoovers. Photograph by Dan Forer.

Opposite: When Wilson undertook the two-year project to restore and renovate the historic 1926 Biltmore Hotel in Coral Gables, Florida, she employed ecclesiastical restorers from Mexico to work on the dramatically vaulted colonnades. Pigments were scraped and examined under a microscope to determine the original colors. Photograph by Karl Francetic.

Overleaf, left: The Coral Gables Golf Club, constructed in 1926, was faithfully restored to its former glory following a fire in the early 1980s. The dining room overlooking the pool is glass-enclosed. Exterior arched openings are washed with light to enhance the architecture. Mexican terra-cotta tiles cover the floors. Photograph by Dan Forer.

Overleaf, right: The renovation of the Boca Raton Hotel and Beach Club, built in 1926, was a seven-year renovation and decoration project. Wilson completed this enormous job in 1990. In the grand entrance lobby, a vaulted timbered ceiling, terra-cotta tile floors, and arched doorways—Mediterranean-style motifs popular in Florida during the 1920s and 1930s—were graciously and meticulously restored. Photograph by Dan Forer.

Left: Built in 1908, and a legendary hotel in the South of France ever since, the Hotel Bel-Air Cap-Ferrat was recently renovated by Wilson & Associates. The design budget hovered near the $10 million mark. In the reception area of the hotel, an antique marble concierge desk was given a fresh look with trompe l'oeil painted panels. Details, such as the wrought-iron shutters, were focused on, and add to the sense of palatial luxury. Antique furnishings were selected to match the Second Empire–style architecture of the building. Photograph by Robert Miller.

Below left: The Game Bar at the Four Seasons Hotel and Resort, an executive conference center in Irving, Texas, provides a club atmosphere in which to relax after a full day of meetings. A cocktail lounge, billiard table, and card tables are provided. A selection of hunting trophies and other art and objects related to sport are displayed. Photograph by Jaime Ardiles-Arce.

Opposite: A sophisticated milieu was deemed appropriate for the top-floor club at the Horizon Condominium in New York City, designed by Trisha Wilson & Associates. Polished marble table tops and comfortable upholstered club chairs orchestrate with a selection of sophisticated works of art to provide the desired atmosphere. Photograph by Jaime Ardiles-Arce.

Top: The internationally renowned St. Andrew's Old Course Hotel in Scotland is a mecca for golfers around the world. In a renovation of the hotel that involved some new construction, Wilson designed a new reception area with slate floors and faux-finish stone walls to create a place that gives visitors a sense of having arrived in a stately manor house. Photograph by Scott MacDonald, Hedrich-Blessing.

Above: The indoor swimming pool and spa area at St. Andrew's offers a mural of a countryside scene in eighteenth-century Scotland. The skylight above the pool assists in creating the effect of a conservatory. Photograph by Scott MacDonald, Hedrich-Blessing.

Right: The Inn of the Anasazi in Santa Fe, New Mexico, brings the majesty and mystery of a long-lost desert culture to a luxury hotel. The wooden ceiling in the library replicates an Anasazi technique. Native American rugs, pots, baskets, and other artifacts give authentic touches to the warm, rustic space. Photograph by Lisl Dennis.

Clodagh

MINIMALISTS

Though Minimalists are most comfortable working

out their ideas in pared-down Modernist style,

with a minimum of ornament, decoration,

and color, their concepts are not necessarily limited

to Bauhaus-style applications. Minimalism

might be redefined in today's terms as simplicity.

With their preferred palette of black, gray,

beige, and white, these designers create neutral

backgrounds against which people

supply the color.

There are interiors that are simply aesthetic arrangements of objects in space, and then there are interiors with an intangible atmosphere beyond their physicality. These atmospheric spaces elicit emotional reactions—feelings of welcome, comfort, mystery, excitement, serenity, happiness, joy. To sit in Clodagh's loft, on the fourth floor of a Manhattan walkup, one floor above her eight-person office space, is to experience all of these feelings. The brick walls are painted white, but are distressed to give the effect of a soft rustication; a fountain sculpture fills the air with the delicate sound of trickling water; intriguing freestanding artworks function as lighting; soft beige leather furniture gathered around a hearth welcomes the sitter; a circular table set with Chinese tableware invites; greenery at the windows delights. Always known in business by her first name only, Clodagh is an exception to almost every rule, yet she is one of the most acclaimed names in the profession, with an international reputation and a list of clients ranging from the largest Japanese advertising agency, Dentsu, to the actors Paul Newman and Joanne Woodward, for whom she designed a loft in Manhattan's Soho. She has been described as being on the leading edge of thinking about environmental ecology and psychology.

Totally unschooled in design, but gifted with a natural genius, Clodagh started off as a fashion designer in Dublin, Ireland, at the age of seventeen, swiftly achieving worldwide recognition, before switching to interior design when she got bored with the fickle and ephemeral nature of clothes in 1974. Her entry into the interiors field occurred completely by happenstance and took place in Spain, where she had gone to sit on a beach and ponder the next phase of her life. Clodagh explains, "I wanted to renovate a townhouse, and the architects that I met seemed to be talking drivel, so I decided to do it myself. I thought, 'What have I got to lose?' I didn't know anything about drawing or layouts, but I had started my fashion business after learning how to cut patterns in three months."

She got into not only architecture and interiors but landscaping to boot, learning her trade "hands on" alongside plumbers, electricians, masons, and other artisans. She found she enjoyed the process and decided to open her own business. Her first customer was a man who wanted to open a restaurant. She completed the job, it was a success, and her career snowballed from there. Her design credo was to "simplify" her clients' lives. (Initially, they were mostly people who wanted low-maintenance vacation homes in Spain.) It was from their needs that she grew to love and to develop what she calls "eroded, pre-aged materials," together with her personal motto: "Why not?"

After six years in Spain, she was ready for a more adventurous arena and chose New York City. In the mid-1980s, New Yorkers were ready to receive Clodagh. "I don't have a look or a style," says Clodagh, although observers may disagree. "I confront people with their own life-styles and make them think about what they want out of their lives. I'm told I'm tough and outspoken. People either like me or they don't." In 1986 Clodagh, with two partners, Ivy Ross and Sherri Williams, opened Clodagh Ross Williams on the newly fashionable Lower East Side. The store featured products designed by artists and craftspeople, including furniture, accessories, and jewelry, jammed together in a casual manner. They were fashioned out of materials such as rusted metals, concrete, and raw-edged granite; the forms were called "New Wave" and were in tune with the then-influential Memphis movement, which had transformed design aesthetics earlier in the decade. While the furnishings looked rather fantastic, they were quite practical and functional, because Clodagh has a passion for "things that work." (The store closed in 1989 at the end of the high-rolling Reagan era.)

Working independently, Clodagh assembled a group of more than forty artists and artisans (many of whom had shown their wares in her shop) with whom she collaborated on several assignments, from the corporate executive offices of the American Can Company, to law offices for Weil, Gotshal & Manges, and a slew of Manhattan residences. "I decided to do general design, not just interior design, anything from a spoon, to a vase, to a skyscraper. I want to change the way people perceive their options. You don't always have to do something one way, just because it has always been done that way," Clodagh explains.

Above: Stairway, Plush/Sally residence, New York City. Photograph by Daniel Aubry.

Her philosophy of design matched the moment. Clodagh offered a new kind of minimalism, without the hard-edge high-tech finish that had been seen before. There was something more personal here, and while it obviously had to do with the individual craftsmanship and artistry that went into the entire project, from door handles, to customized kitchen counters, sometimes made of concrete edged with stainless steel, to plaster walls with metallic

Above: Entrance vestibule, Harrison penthouse, New York City. Photograph by Daniel Aubry.

color rubbed into them to give a dull sheen, it went beyond the objects. Clodagh herself believes it has to do with her interest in spiritual dimensions: "I was born in Oscar Wilde's old home in County Mayo. My childhood was connected with fairy rings, myths, and legends, the Book of Kells, superstition, drama, nannies who told ghost stories. If you brought the wrong flower into the house, it had to be exorcised. Later in life I discovered yoga, Buddhism, and other Eastern philosophies, including feng shui, the ancient Chinese art of geomancy and placement. I am convinced of the power of invisible energy patterns and vibrations and the concept of using these elements for positive health and well-being within and around spaces and buildings. The use of these kinds of natural resources seems to be overlooked. In Europe people thought I was a crank when I talked about interior design as a healing art; in America they accept it."

Clodagh's clients are likely to be initiated into ideas about storage, garbage disposal, and respect for ecology, together with the most sophisticated video and audio communications. She experiments with state-of-the-art fiber optics and uses each job as a laboratory for testing out the latest technological thinking. The clients will also be drilled into understanding the value of the unfinished. "The danger of the homogenized finished room is a characterlessness," claims the designer. "An unfinished appearance makes it look as if some kind of energy can still happen."

Clodagh's major preoccupation now is establishing her Center for American Design, an ambitious, million-dollar store in Soho representing more than 200 artists. It will be an educational center as well as a place to shop, exposing customers to the artists and their thought and design processes. She feels the public deserves the opportunity "to grow." With this project, Clodagh is typically riding the new wave for the nineties.

A selection of Clodagh's work appears on pages 128 to 131.

Carol **Groh**

Reactions to feng shui, the ancient Chinese art of placement, can be positive, negative, or somewhere in between. Students of this art believe that the placement of windows, doors, and furniture in a space, even the smallest objects in a room, can have an effect on the spirit of the interior, with fortunate—or unfortunate—results. Feng shui does not apply just to interiors. Exterior placement, or siting, of buildings can be equally fortuitous, or not, depending on the structure's relationship to the natural elements of earth, wind, and water, and the four cardinal points—north, south, east, and west. A recent debate involving feng shui centers around the building placements in Hong Kong of the Bank of Shanghai and Hong Kong, designed by British architect Norman Foster, and the Bank of China, by Chinese-American architect I. M. Pei. Foster consulted feng-shui experts; Pei did not. Pei's octagonal, glass-sheathed skyscraper has been cited by local people as having such bad feng shui that many who live and work in surrounding buildings have placed mirrors on the outside of their walls, to deflect the bad energy thrown off by the skyscraper. Foster's building, by contrast, is respected and favored for its good vibrations and positive *ch'i* (energy).

Carol Groh, president of Carol Groh & Associates, is a designer who has been employing feng shui since she reformed her own business in 1986, after separating from a business partner, Robert Najarian, with whom she had worked for seven years. Deciding that the spirit of her firm must reflect the feminine moniker of its president, she concentrated on establishing signals of healing and nurturing, with the objective of helping her clients "to grow and to flourish." She recalls, "I said to Thomas Mahoney, my design associate, 'Let's look at the concepts of feng shui and incorporate them into the planning concepts of our offices and the overall image of the company.' It was a symbolic approach, a way of bringing the firm together." She began by having her New York offices analyzed by a feng-shui expert, Sarah Rossbach. When Rossbach first walked into the firm's headquarters, she noted that the placement of the front desk suggested there might be a problem keeping a receptionist. "It was true," admitted Groh. "We did, but we couldn't figure out how Sarah Rossbach would know!" It turned out that the entrance of the office opened directly onto the receptionist's desk, leaving her exposed to negative *ch'i*. Moving the desk and installing a mirror behind it helped to "cure" this situation.

Groh's current offices are a model example of feng shui, which, according to Rossbach, a disciple of the Chinese feng-shui guru Professor Lin Yun, helps to establish an environment that is comfortable, bright, and spacious with no oppressive feelings that impede good health, positive energy, or positive thinking. Such attention to placement results in the betterment and advancement of individual and collective prosperity.

Key to a successful business is the placement of the president's desk, which should keep a chief executive in view and command of all. "It's crucial to the outcome of the company," declares Rossbach. Heeding her mentor's advice, Groh

Above: President's office, Warner Communications, New York City. Photograph by Durston Saylor.

dispensed with doors on all the executive offices, allowing free-flowing accessibility to the design studio. The firm's conference room has doors that fold away when client meetings demanding privacy are not in progress. An appropriate sense of hierarchy was also planned into the space, with designers and middle managers understanding the pecking order through the placement of their workstations, without any obvious graphic communication. The entry from the elevator lobby resembles a gate, with subtle lighting and a mirror helping to give "good feelings" to those who pass through this portal. Pale pastel colors—peach, gray, and green—wash the walls "to avoid an all-white envelope" and are carried through onto the firm's graphic communications. "The variety of colors help us to change continually, as we feel we want to, symbolizing growth," notes Groh. "They also convey a sense of harmony, because they look good together." She adds that the more she learns about feng shui, a concept dating back thousands of years, the more she understands that the philosophy is about elements designers practice all the time, very often by instinct.

This search for something beyond the expected has manifested itself throughout Groh's career. Born and raised in Grand Rapids, Michigan, she spent two years at Hillsdale College in Michigan and then struck out for New York to pursue an education in design. She studied at New York University, earning a Bachelor of Arts degree in 1965, and Parsons, where she obtained an environmental design degree in 1966. Returning to the Midwest, she landed a job at Skidmore Owings & Merrill, Chicago. Groh recalls, "I'd always wanted to work there but never thought I'd be accepted." In fact, the firm was impressed to find a woman who understood the realities of design, including how to handle specifications. For Groh, SOM presented an opportunity to work with one of the most stimulating design teams in the country in the late 1960s, a group that included Jack Dunbar, Margo Grant, Robert Kleinschmidt, Donald Powell, Margaret McCurry, Charles Pfister, and Davis Allen. She credits Allen in particular as "[having] had so much to give in terms of his knowledge and patience with young people." Groh worked with Allen on the design of the Lyndon Johnson Library and learned "how to listen to clients and to what they expect . . . and remember that you are designing for the client and not for yourself. Dave taught me that however good your ideas are, they may not be right for the client."

In her three years at SOM, Chicago, she learned about design and its relation to the business world, and in 1971 was delighted to be transferred to the New York office, where she rose to associate partner. A marriage to SOM partner Don Smith led her to establish her own company in 1979, in order to avoid a conflict of interest.

Careful review of the options when starting a new, small firm in New York led Groh to ponder several issues. "One of the most problematic aspects of running a design firm is that very few designers ever learn to be businesspeople," she says. "Firms that can't get ahead haven't taken a serious look at this need." Clients require a sense of economy and an understanding of real estate, along with an awareness of marketing, she adds. Groh defined her service, chose a target market, sized up the competition, marketed her company, and put financial and management systems in place. An initial $20,000 contract with Deloitte Haskins & Sells set up an entire accounting system, which has been in place since day one, along with advice that included a strict warning not to continue to work on a project if the client had not paid outstanding service fees within ninety days. "It was tough advice, but it works," says Groh. "And it's the only thing to do if you want to survive and prosper in today's tough market." She also found the seminars at the American Woman's Economic Development and the National Association of Women in Business Organization helpful.

Her business plan defines her niche as a boutique operation, offering an extremely strong sense of planning and space evaluation, allied with a reputation for creative interiors executed with strict cost control. Her market is Fortune 500 corporations. From a start-up staff of three, Groh's firm quickly mushroomed to a staff of fifteen, with a growing list of clients, including General Electric, fashion designer Carolyne Roehm, J. P. Stevens, Random House, and Chase Manhattan Bank. The professionalism of her firm and its businesslike diversity (she went into graphics programs and product design for Geiger, HBF, Larson, Bernhardt, David Edward, and BPC to balance out ebbs and flows in interiors business) led her to be selected as the first female Designer of the Year by *Interiors* in 1988.

Unique to her marketing approach has been her concentration on top corporate projects, jobs which other boutique firms would consider impossible to get. Groh reasoned that these companies most often employed educated facilities managers with a strong sense and awareness of design. She also concluded that if she was successful with these clients there would be repeat business, instead of a one-time involvement, thus saving her money and effort in marketing. This strategy, too, has worked. General Electric, for example, has returned for a number of different projects over the past thirteen years.

Although Groh loves to devote time to hands-on drawing and design, she has learned that 80 percent of her job is administrative. Building harmonious relationships with clients is probably more important than anything. She always starts with the CEO, trying to create confidence by gathering information about the company and establishing appropriate symbolic motifs and images in the project's design. Groh asserts, "This is the way you sell a specific design. It has to be unique."

Balancing this brisk, financially oriented "yang" methodology is exquisite work in minimalist style, executed with a feminine "ying" touch. Rich detailing in materials and finishes orchestrates an ambience of serenity and simplicity. Recessed lighting and built-in furniture control spaces. Harmony is created with a reductive use of objects and furnishings. If a client is looking for fashion, then Groh is not the firm. "The whole thrust is that we want a design that's lasting, that our clients will be proud of ten years from now."

A selection of Groh's work appears on pages 132 to 135.

WILLIAM WHITEHURST

Margaret **Helfand**

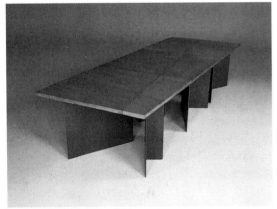

Above: The Table in Six Segments, made of garnet-blasted bent steel and maple plywood with bronze dust finish, separates into trapezoidal sections that can be reconfigured to create various geometric forms. The table was designed by Margaret Helfand with Marti Cowan. Photograph by Philip Thompson.

Walking into Margaret Helfand's New York office in an East Side brownstone, there is no doubt that this designer is a nonconformist. In what was once the parlor-floor dining room, with its paneled walls and marble fireplace, is now a peculiarly angular table, ten feet long, with a top of inexpensive fiberboard astride a corrugated platform, resting on a steel base. The eight chairs surrounding the table are made of textured bent steel, all in different shapes. They look strangely elegant, fragile, and uncomfortable, but in fact they are as comfortable as any other side chair without the benefit of cushioned upholstery.

This room serves as a conference space as well as Helfand's office. Her desk, another angular custom-made design, is placed along one wall. The powerful visual ensemble introduces clients to the firm's outlook. Raw elements—stone, metal, glass, wood—and simple structural systems are the common denominators in all of Helfand's work. Frequently irregular and unexpected forms are generated by context, program requirements, or method of construction. It is, according to Helfand, a highly rational approach to design, which seeks a new sense of order from within the process of design and construction itself, rather than relying on the traditional sources of historical forms or preconceived theoretical ideas. The articulation of this philosophy has met with considerable recognition, including AIA and other awards, invitations to speak at universities, and the opportunity to serve on the prestigious board of officers of the New York chapter of the AIA—an organization that does not mingle with renegades too often.

Where did this renegade spirit come from? Surely not from a conventional design-school education. Helfand's background and the history of her introduction to the fields of interiors, furniture, and architecture are as irregular as her designs themselves. After studying art history at Swarthmore, she enrolled at the UC Berkeley architecture school in the late 1960s, at the time of the student revolutions. During her first year, claims Helfand, she hardly had time for architectural studies—she was too busy demonstrating and politicking, basking in the heady rhetoric of the era that proclaimed architecture was going to change the world. Nevertheless, the California environment in which she was raised, with its predilection for basic building and materials, had a subconscious impact. A trip to

London introduced her to some other revolutionaries—the Archigram team headed by Peter Cook—and she decided to stay there for a year and pursue her education at the Architectural Association.

After England came Spain, and her first experience at building from the inside out. Helfand and a group of twenty friends bought a ninety-foot three-masted schooner for $1,500 and decided to make it seaworthy enough to cross the Atlantic. According to Helfand, "I felt this was the best experience I could have, learning the trades and understanding how something was built. We did everything, fabricating steel rigging, electrical and mechanical work, cabinetmaking, all the things that can seem very intimidating to an architect if you haven't actually done them. Now I enjoy going out on construction sites because I understand the trades thoroughly and love getting involved with them and solving problems. Someone who can do this with a tradesman feeds back into the design process."

Helfand notes that aside from forcing her to learn the skills hands-on, this shipbuilding and sailing odyssey across the Mediterranean, Atlantic, Caribbean, and Pacific, which took up three years of her life, taught her that she could do anything she wanted. Upon returning to port in San Francisco and Berkeley in 1973, she finished up her architecture degree and embarked on her professional career. By 1976 she was in New York working for Marcel Breuer Associates, whose founder was a "hero" she most admired for his reductive rationale and use of honest, basic materials. Soon she was involved with big projects such as an electrical power station and visitor's center on the Savannah River, and the Atlanta Central Library, for which she drew full-size construction details. She earned the honor of being made the first woman architectural associate in the firm.

In 1981 she was ready to go out on her own, with a small staff. Typically, Helfand will have up to twelve projects on the boards at a time, ranging from apartment or house interiors, to commercial, retail, and institutional projects. But whatever comes her way, it will receive the same treatment—a very rigorous aesthetic, derived, she believes, from her interest in Eastern religion. As she puts it, "You don't need a lot to make things wonderful. There is an aesthetic of tranquility in Japanese design, which has to do with rigorous geometry being allied to restfulness and repose, to ensure well-being." This search for simplicity and tranquility, she adds, should be just right "for life in the 1990s. Excess has always made me nervous. We experienced that in the 1980s. Now we are weeding out. I have found life to be best when it's very simple. This is the way you relate to the universe."

Working three dimensionally within the architectural

Above: Café W chairs and table, designed by Margaret Helfand. Photograph by Tom Bonner.

envelope, Helfand is involved in every facet of a project and almost always custom designs the furniture and lighting. For her residential clients, tables are usually unique and unusually flexible, made with up to six pieces that can be used together or apart, allowing for varied configurations. Lighting fixtures are constructed of glass and metal, to incorporate her favorite halogen bulbs. She explains that she is "forced into designing them, because there is so little I like on the market, and what is there is too expensive."

Helfand's meticulous inquiries into how things work and her insistence on detailing lead her to investigate issues on many different levels in the profession. One constant inquiry is why there is so little respect for or awareness of the value of architecture and design by the public. She feels this has to do with the fact that most designers lack the time to project an image or to help educate the public. "They're all so busy just trying to earn a living, consumed by their practice, working seven days a week, twelve hours a day, that they forget or simply can't get to the public issues," she says. "But the profession is suffering from neglecting these issues. Architects and designers have not made themselves as highly valued as they should be. The public doesn't appreciate them." In an effort to try and change this perception, she initiated a Long Range Plan, published by the AIA's New York chapter, which encompasses three goals: Design Excellence, Professional Development, and Public Outreach.

To implement these goals, various committees have been established, with mandates to generate appropriate activities. For example, public outreach activities range from assuming leadership in public policy issues, to communicating the value of the profession, to advocating the benefits of the profession in terms of legislative issues. There are recommendations, too, for hiring public-relations consultants to formulate strategy, encourage public membership in the AIA, and expand media exposure into consumer print and even cable television.

Having produced this formidable document, Helfand is now off the AIA board after a four-year term and back in touch with her own firm, spending more of her time on the exquisite details that give her the inner satisfaction she wants from her career. "The rewards will never be financial or come from believing that you can change the world radically," she declares. "I can't say that 100 percent of my energy goes into efforts to improve the external universe, but there is an important reward on an internal level of enjoying the art of what I do and deriving pleasure from creating places and elements that have a life and integrity of their own."

A selection of Helfand's work appears on pages 136 to 139.

GERALD RATTO

Carolyn **Iu**

Above: Mock-up of general office space for the Chase Manhattan Bank at Metrotech, Brooklyn, New York, a two-million-square-foot project. Photograph by Ken Ritter.

I f there is one major corporate office project that expresses commercial interior design of the 1980s, it is Merrill Lynch's world headquarters in the World Financial Center at Battery Park City in New York. Opening just prior to the "Black Monday" crash of 1987, this four-million-square-foot, twenty-eight-floor project by Skidmore Owings & Merrill was destined to represent the end of an era. There would be no more financial corporations of comparable magnitude emerging. The world of Wall Street and financial tycoonery was shattered by lawsuits and criminal proceedings, and its bigger-than-life, over-the-top deal making was mercilessly exposed in Tom Wolfe's *Bonfire of the Vanities.*

The Merrill skyscraper was designed to house 14,000-plus employees, previously scattered over more than eleven different sites. Three state-of-the-art trading rooms accommodated literally thousands of traders, each positioned with a battery of up to six monitors before him, interfacing with global financial centers by satellite. And on three executive floors, the private offices for the "top brass," along with conference rooms, boardroom, and twelve private dining rooms, displayed museum-quality art in a clublike atmosphere of fine wood paneling, silk-covered sofas, and subdued lighting.

Carolyn Iu spent four years of her life on this project, working under the managing partner, Raul de Armas—two years on the relocation plan and scheduling strategy and two more years on the design of the myriad interior spaces, which included fitness centers, medical units, and an employee cafeteria, all offered as evidence that the corporation had a commitment to design, as well as to caring for its human resources. Iu and de Armas had a common background—both were Cornell graduates—although Iu studied at the Department of Environmental Design and de Armas at the School of Architecture. Iu graduated in 1975 as one of six women in a class of eighty, but she never felt the odds were against her. "I've been one of the lucky ones," she claims. "I've been able to pursue my career as a woman and have never felt that I had to be like a man. I don't believe I have been held back in any way. However, I have often wondered whether it would be different if I was actually doing architecture."

Iu knew that she wanted to work at SOM, but when she arrived in New York from Ithaca she found they were laying off, not hiring, so she took a plane to San Francisco. Born in Hong Kong, she hoped she would feel at home in this city, with its large Chinese-American population—and she did. When her working permit expired in 1977, she was on her way to Europe, but stopped in New York and met an immigration lawyer at a party who said he could help her obtain a green card. She stayed on, found the recession had lifted, and got herself the job she wanted at SOM, New York. At that time work was ongoing in Saudi Arabia, and she was put on the team for the King Abdul

Above: The Palio leather desk accessories collection designed by Iu and SOM associate Raul de Armas, manufactured by The Knoll Group. Photograph courtesy of The Knoll Group.

Aziz International Airport in Jidda, a gargantuan structure known as the Haj Terminal. The terminal totaled more than 9 million square feet, with more than 550 million square feet of paved, surface-treated, and landscaped areas. SOM big guns Gordon Bunschaft, Carolina Woo, Carol Groh, and Davis Allen were all trained on this blockbuster, which was to win the firm numerous awards. Iu's contribution as a junior designer was noted and she went on to work with Allen on the fifty-two-story Georgia-Pacific headquarters in Atlanta, the new SOM offices in New York, the 1-million-square-foot headquarters for Irving Trust in New York, and Paine Webber's New York corporate headquarters before being assigned to Merrill Lynch in 1986. She has nothing but praise for Allen: "Dave is patient and fun, and teaches without teaching. He has such a sense of balance. He is able to trigger thoughts and transform the simplest things. I saw how he strived for that Japanese sense of serenity in everything he did."

"I'm glad I went through the eighties," reflects Iu. "It was a time of growth for everyone. Certainly at SOM the partners all learned to appreciate interiors." The Skidmore methodology has always separated responsibilities, dividing a job team into three parts: the designer, who comes up with the design concept, "sells" it, and implements it; the project manager, responsible for the budget and day-to-day billing; and the job captain, in charge of the technical responsibilities and the construction documentation. Now, after fifteen years in the firm, Iu has risen to associate partner, a promotion that recognizes her management and leadership qualities. In 1991 she moved to the San Francisco office, to take charge of the interior design department there as well as the firm's interiors team in Los Angeles. With limits placed on construction and development in San Francisco, the design market in the future is going to be more interiors oriented, so Iu's brief is to build a strong team on the West Coast. "But we're not going to get huge," she insists. "I feel many students don't want to work at SOM because they believe they will get lost. That is not the

case. We do huge jobs, but we have fewer people than we used to. Where we once had a hundred people we now have forty. Computers have helped us to streamline our operation."

To broaden her qualifications, Iu recently determined to become a registered architect, passing the eight-part National Council of Architectural Registration Boards exam, which she was qualified to take as a result of her long-standing apprenticeship in an architectural firm. "I would have gone into architecture at the very beginning—my grandfather was an architect—but I was scared of the structures aspect and the math, calculus, and physics," explains Iu. She adds that many people question her decision to add this architectural qualification, at a time when the practice of interior design has been legislated into a legitimate profession. "People ask me why I'm not content to be an interior designer and be proud of that. I have a big reason. I don't think that interior design education is good enough for the work that is going on today. There is a huge gap between architecture and interiors in terms of what is taught. Furniture and finishes are not enough. Of course there are some interior design schools that teach more than that, but so often they do so without understanding structures and architecture. Working in an architecture firm helped me to learn what I was not taught at school. I understood that I needed to study structures, do calculus, and come to grips with the basics of technical, mechanical, and electrical systems."

With her new status, Iu is set for the coveted promotion to partner, which has been conferred on just six women in the fifty-eight-year history of the prestigious firm, where male partners currently number twenty-five and have even been as high as forty-four when the going was good. Iu confesses she never set this as a goal, but still it seems appropriate for someone who admits she began building in the nursery—"not small things but big cities."

A selection of Iu's work appears on pages 140 to 143.

LUCA VIGNELLI

Stephanie **Mallis**

Above: Ballroom, The John B. Hynes Veterans Memorial Convention Center, Boston, Massachusetts. Photograph by Peter Vanderwarker.

It is well after normal working hours, but on the thirty-seventh floor of the Chrysler Building, in the heart of midtown Manhattan, there is still a buzz of activity. Stephanie Mallis and her three associates, packed into a compact 1,000 square feet, with a vista of twinkling towers surrounding them, are at the drawing boards and on the computer, working on their biggest project so far in the five-year history of this micro company. It is a mammoth (450,000-square-foot) office interior for Becton Dickinson, a corporate campus in New Jersey, begun in 1986, which has won numerous awards for its architecture by the Kallmann McKinnell & Wood firm of Boston. Mallis insists the project is well within the firm's capacity. "It's true that most small offices generally do small jobs. The fact is that the same problems exist whether you are designing for one person or 1,200 people, if you are trying to fit an individual into a desk," she points out.

Of course, Mallis has had the advantage of working for big architecture firms—Skidmore Owings & Merrill, Rogers Butler & Bergun Architects (now Butler Rogers Baskett), Payette Associates Architects, and I. M. Pei & Partners—and she knows all the nuances involved in handling a major client such as Becton Dickinson. What is more, she has never chosen the conventional route along her career path and is known for her drive toward excellence, as demonstrated in the golden Big I *Interiors* award sitting on her window ledge, which she won in 1990 for her interiors of the Boston Convention Center.

After graduating from Pratt Institute with a bachelor of fine arts honors degree in 1967, Mallis spent the first ten years of her career firmly rooted in interior design. It was the burgeoning era of high-tech, platformed apartments and "living differently" (e.g., single-parent households, loft living)—generated partly by the sexual revolution. Influenced by designer Ward Bennett, for whom she worked briefly, she fell naturally into this spare, pared-down mode and had her work published in numerous shelter magazines. Her own apartment in I. M. Pei's then-brand-new Kips Bay Towers exemplified the look, with freestanding dividers and platformed areas upholstered in industrial gray carpeting.

But ten years later she found she was frustrated working around people who were highly qualified and tended to tell her that she was not. "I decided to go and learn more, because I needed to move on," she says. She applied to the architecture schools at Columbia, Yale, and Harvard, finally settling on Harvard because Gerald McCue was dean and the school had recently begun hiring first-rate guest critics, including Michael Graves, Richard Meier, Harry Cobb, Michael McKinnell, and Charles Kallmann. "I studied with them because I liked their work, and I knew the school had more of an interest in architectural issues than in stylistic issues," notes Mallis.

Though it wasn't easy being a mature student (she was in her thirties), Mallis finished the three-and-a-half-year course in two years, graduating with a masters in 1978. She received a Fulbright scholarship in architecture and traveled through Europe for a third year of education in 1979, "to look at the things I'd been taught about, delve into history, and investigate sites." Upon returning, she was asked by her Harvard professor, Harry Cobb, partner at I. M. Pei (now Pei Cobb Freed & Partners), to join the firm as an architect but to focus on the interior design of big buildings—the Bank of China in Hong Kong, the Mobil Exploration and Production Research Laboratory in Texas, IBM's office buildings in Purchase and Somers, New York, and in Philadelphia, and Mount Sinai Hospital in New York City were some of the major projects that came her way.

Mallis's previous design experience gave her a unique insight into these assignments. The tables were now turned: she was an architect but was familiar with the design of interior space as well. This was a challenging responsibility that put all of her skills to the test. "It wasn't about Vivien's shoe closet," she notes with a smile, alluding to her previous residential experiences. It was more about connections between macro and micro—for example, taking the stone used in the base of the building and using it as a top for a cafeteria table, or getting inside the head of a person using an open-plan workstation, making a person feel comfortable within 500 square feet of personal territory in a high-rise building that could sometimes feel overwhelming.

As Mallis took more and more of a lead in the firm's interiors work, the department grew. After seven years she was director of interior design, heading up a corps of twenty people, and the firm's portfolio of building types had developed from the special art museums and institutional work for which it had a worldwide reputation to hotels and corporate headquarters. It was Mallis's particular responsibility to make sense of a building type in which many floors were designed with repetitive elements. In every job, the "ulterior motive" was the notion of uplifting the spirit, making the people using the building feel connected with grand architecture that resonated on many experiential levels. "You put more into large commercial projects because people are going to enjoy them for some time," Mallis explains. "With personal spaces, people come and go—with divorce, for example."

Despite the prestige and recognition that accrued while working for the high-profile Pei firm, and the elevation to associate partner, Mallis was discontented. She longed to get back to the drawing board, to put her own hands on design, and to be in charge of her own destiny, as opposed to seeing and critiquing other people's design ideas. She went solo "with no backup, no funds, definitely not the way you do it if you read books about how to start a business." Her assistant joined her from Pei, and she started work on the John B. Hynes Convention Center in Boston, as a design consultant in collaboration with her former professor, Michael McKinnell of Kallmann McKinnell & Wood.

As her association with the firm progressed, she was called in on the United States Chancery and Marine Guard Quarters in Dacca, Bangladesh, the Harvard University School of Business Administration Athletic Facilities Complex in Cambridge, Massachusetts, the Groton School renovation and addition, and the United States Embassy in Bangkok, Thailand. "They do outstanding work, but they are also very demanding," she says of Kallmann McKinnell & Wood. But clearly the two firms, the macro and the micro, have developed a symbiotic relationship. Mallis's approach to the Convention Center, for example, was to establish more welcoming spaces and a friendlier atmosphere than is usual in such large facilities. She called for unconventional approaches to lighting, insisted on the softness of draperies and large expanses of glazing, and installed high-style modern furniture to create the appropriate sense of ritual in the public meeting and ceremonial rooms.

Meanwhile, word-of-mouth recommendations led to other independent commissions, including the New York headquarters of Planned Parenthood, a dress boutique in Texas, and an apartment in New York.

If Mallis has a signature, it is in the way she brings as much custom work and originality as she can to corporate projects. Often clients won't ask for special furniture, but she finds that she can convince them to agree to this approach through presentations that demonstrate efficiency. She believes that "a corporate building should not inevitably be about buying from a catalog. To express the best of the architecture you must abstract from that design." This approach is amply conveyed in the interiors of a second Becton Dickinson building, for which she won the contract by diligent investigation and research, going out and photographing the site, presenting ideas and photographic collages that emanated from the first building on the campus. Thus, the landscape's patterns of grasses were incorporated via her office computer into designs for custom carpeting. And her inquiries into the nature of the computerized work force produced a brand-new concept for a workstation—a sweeping, continuous work surface designed to accommodate the array of equipment now at every employee's service. The most successful results, she insists, do not come out of our own attitudes but from something that's already there. "That's when something new happens."

A selection of Mallis's work appears on pages 144 to 147.

Elizabeth McClintock

Elizabeth McClintock is a self-confessed reformed rebel, and her biography certainly confirms her record as an unconventional architect and designer. At nineteen, while a student at McGill University in Canada, she spent four months on Baffin Island in a government research group, living in an Eskimo community of 2,000 single men and 5 women. She has traveled to every continent except Australia. She has climbed mountains in the Himalayas, the Andes, and the Atlas, where she trekked alone on horseback along dirt roads for four weeks, crossing into the Sahara and living in Berber villages. She has a passion for skydiving and for training racehorses—in short, for living dangerously. What does all this have to do with architecture and design, specifically with being a partner in one of the most successful small firms in New York, MGS Architects, whose design for the restaurant America was written up in a record twenty publications?

McClintock has no trouble explaining. She gets her best ideas in the mountains, she says, and every trip is a learning experience: "I learn about people and the way the world works. Even local people in the Third World—when I am right there sleeping, sometimes not even in a sleeping bag—have something to teach me. In this situation the game of meeting people becomes a lot more important. I crave this stimulation, meeting new people. I believe mental health and well-being are based on a proper level of stimulation. In modern life, most of us go around understimulated, unexposed to danger, not having to fight over food, or sex." Travel, along with the act of being engaged in geography and mapping, she adds, is also a help in understanding how building elements—earth, rock, sand, and water—get put together, to resolve destinations, to develop a sense of order.

Becoming involved in life's dramas is perhaps a natural outcome, she believes, of her very conservative background and religious upbringing, which included little exposure to people and a protected East Coast schooling. "She describes herself as a tomboy who saw that "men had more adventures and more independence than women. I wanted boy skills and boy daring so that I would have an interesting life, too." She rebelliously chose to attend Canada's McGill University because it was out of the country and "seemed like an adventure." And she has been adventuring ever since. She briefly tried acting out her zest for dramatics in the theater but later returned to Pratt Institute, followed by Yale for her master's in architecture.

It was at Pratt that she first found a mentor whose thinking matched her own in terms of the search for the unconventional: William Fogler. "He thought of space in three layers—static, dynamic, and organic—and had us do three-dimensional exercises for each," recalls McClintock. "He taught me how to stimulate people with design on a visceral level." Haresh Lalvani was also influential. He taught an unusual structures course in which organic forms such as animal limbs were analyzed as models and then developed into designs for bridges, towers, and long-span roofs based on the principals observed.

At Yale, King Lui Wu was another teacher who inspired her with his sensitivity and his insistence on the use of natural daylight. "He was not a high-profile critic. For him, style was nondescript. He liked my crude, unusual designs. He taught little about the refinements of architecture, but he taught very important principles." It was at Yale that she met her partner, Anthony Grammenopoulos.

Believing that architecture and design should be about a hands-on building process, and having worked as a job captain rebuilding her father's workshop in Connecticut, McClintock felt like a misfit at one of her first jobs at Skidmore Owings & Merrill, where she was tied to a drafting board and found the work she was asked to do on two hotels "totally boring." She stayed a brief year and left with the feeling, since modified, that she could never work in the corporate world. She founded her own firm in 1980 and from then on, she says, "things started to go right. I found my energy didn't have to be spent on rebelling but could be spent on design."

Right from the start her work attracted coverage by the media. Though she herself thought of it as "almost baroque," Ernie's, a restaurant on the Upper West Side of Manhattan, caught everyone's attention with its stark austerity: raw brick and paint-splattered walls, bare light bulbs over a conspicuous row of pay telephones giving a signal that "in" dining places didn't have to be outfitted with discrete pink tablecloths and upholstered banquettes. The bar was delineated with a crown of reproduction plaster cornices—the baroque element—and the floor tiled with crisp black-and-white pavers, reminiscent of locker-room showers. The total ensemble—historic elements, dramatic lighting, exposed mechanical ducts, and other "tech"—was seen as a fresh approach "without formulas." To McClintock it was merely a case of looking at the psychological factors "the whole ride, the whole way. We determined that people needed to be jostled out of time and place. The urban archaeology of rough-textured walls, decorative richness, despite the concrete, and architectural relics proved to be comforting and played on people's interest in nostalgia."

Ernie's was the first of seven major dining establishments that earned McClintock and her partners (M and G were joined by William Soloway, making MGS) praise from the critics, notoriety in the public eye, and kudos from clients, who bathed in the success of their enterprises, in a business known for its trendiness and short-lived life spans. For her, the field of restaurant design provided the perfect opportunity to exploit her talent for emotional engagements within an interior. "I think you could argue that it is a woman's point of view that when you do a building the purpose is not to sit outside and look at it," she comments. "For me, the outside can look quite awkward and wild. I want to look past what it is on the outside. It's what it's like on the inside that counts."

With America, she was offered her most stimulating brief: "a big, exciting restaurant where people are entertained by each other." Located in a nineteenth-century building with a cast-iron façade that had once been a department store,

America exploits the senses, with a variety of floor levels, a processional aisle lit with projections of stars, and swirls of red, white, and blue neon overhead, like an elongated flag. Mistily painted illuminated images of the Statue of Liberty, an eagle, a locomotive, and segments of Indian sand paintings cover the walls. McClintock pressed the patriotic theme to the hilt and describes the assemblage as "making it harder to case the joint. I wanted to create attention so that the effects are engaging you and you can't let go, and it's harder to sum up where you are."

McClintock's experience is not limited to restaurants, however. Residential, commercial, and institutional work, including a retirement community project and a boutique hotel, have all come into the office, and she applies the same philosophy to them all: "inventing and being original. I'm never too scared to go into new territory." She has never found that active marketing works for her. "Having an inconveniently old-fashioned education, I believe that, like a woman hoping for a proposal, we should make our work as attractive as possible and wait." Because the firm has low overhead—it is housed in a downtown loft space and has only four people (sometimes stretched to seven as work demands) on the payroll—this unconventional attitude does not court disaster. Furthermore, it allows for serendipitous encounters—like sitting next to a dinner partner at the Explorer's Club annual banquet, who volunteered that he needed a designer to renovate two dormitories for foster-care children. Needless to say, McClintock got the job.

Above: Promostyl fashion industry showroom, New York City. Photograph by Alex Timchula.

A selection of McClintock's work appears on pages 148 to 151.

CHRISTIAN STEINER

Sylvia **Owen**

ylvia Owen's career seems to have followed a charmed path. As a young graduate of the University of Munich in the 1960s, she came to New York City and joined the Knoll Planning Unit, which was then the center of commercial interior design in America. The firm, under the direction of Lewis Butler, a disciple of Florence Knoll, was right next to the offices of Skidmore Owings & Merrill, and it wasn't long before Owen had made friends with the SOM people working on interiors. She steeped herself in the SOM aesthetic of flawless design, which had become the hallmark for corporate design from the 1950s on. "Those were the days when money was not that much of an object," Owen recalls. "We did extraordinary things. If a custom desk, for example, didn't look right, we simply made another. When textiles were needed, Knoll simply went all over Europe finding them. It was quite unusual and it was all wonderful."

By 1971 she was working at John Carl Warnecke, where her understanding of interiors and color, along with a sophisticated eye for art, caught the attention of the founding partner. Owen was the child of a German opera diva and a world-famous American yachtsman, and had been brought up in an artistic European household. "Jack" Warnecke (now retired on the West Coast) became her mentor. Owen describes him as "a person who can think way ahead, in very big terms. He was friends with the Kennedys, he knew the Shah of Iran, he was an incredible socializer. He taught me how to deal with big projects." Warnecke was another hive of design activity in the years she was there. Eugene Kohn, William Pedersen, Shelley Fox, and Patricia Conway, later to form Kohn Pedersen Fox and Kohn Pedersen Fox Conway, were on the boards, along with Emily Malino and Ellen McCluskey, who were later to launch their own interior design firms. After she won an Institute for Business Designers (IBD) first prize award in 1976, Warnecke made her a founding partner of Innerplan, a partnership formed by him and others within the main firm, to specialize in interiors. Owen teamed up in this venture with Anthony Mandolfo (still her associate today) and John Springer. The partnership lasted four years; then "it was time for me to go on. I wanted a larger percentage," says Owen candidly. "Fortunately, Jack understood my feelings and we are still good friends today. Tony Mandolfo and I spoke the same language. He had been at SOM

Above: Soho branch, Chase Manhattan Bank, New York City, Owen & Mandolfo, Inc; senior designer: Lawrence E. Charity. Photograph by Peter Paige.

for fourteen years before Warnecke. We loved working with each other."

One of the partnership's assignments was a shoe store for the French company Charles Jourdan, located on Manhattan's Fifth Avenue. It was to be an anchor corner boutique in the Trump Tower and a prototype for a worldwide company image. The shop was designed with an award-winning ceiling (with a wood grid and recessed lighting), and chairs with leather slipcovers, which gave the store the appropriate aura of glitz and luxury that customers expected. This design also caught the eye of Donald Trump and some of his other tenants, and soon she was working on offices for the Trump Organization and other retail merchants in the vertical shopping complex. In all, Owen's firm designed seventeen stores in Trump Tower. The Christian Dior company was next. For the first Dior boutique in the United States, at Bal Harbor, Florida, the brief was to take the Dior colors (gray and white) but use them in an unconventional way. Her solution was the introduction of gold-rubbed cabinets for merchandise display.

Owen noted the changing design signals in the eighties: "In the seventies we had been very classic and very modern, very Miesian. Now we were becoming more exploratory. We believed in design and we splurged. Unfortunately, people got tired of Postmodernism very quickly, but I think we were working in other directions as well. Unfortunately, by the nineties we had lost a lot of design value. Too many firms went over budget in their explorations; they were poorly informed about technology and business procedures."

In the nineties Owen & Mandolfo are pursuing a more conservative clientele, and they have made a practice of specializing in financial design. Their client list includes ten major banking institutions, from the Chase Manhattan to the Dime, from the Commerzbank to Goldman Sachs. Today, in fact, banks constitute about 80 percent of the firm's business. The rest is composed of retail stores—Davidoff of Geneva is a worldwide client—and some residential work for major clients, often done in joint-venture with prominent architectural firms.

Owen has gained a reputation for her classic work. "We know our clients do not want to be bored after a few years. We avoid anything trendy," she notes. After living for two decades in a twentieth-century modern house on Block Island, off the coast of Rhode Island, Owen recently bought a Greek revival farmhouse in New York's Hudson River Valley, which reflects a whole new sensibility. It caught the eye of the editors at *Architectural Digest* and admitted her to their prestigious list of 100 architects for 1990. Immersed as she is in stylish corporate and retail interiors, the house is a more traditional background for a notable collection of modern art by Christo, Louise Nevelson, Joan Miró, Henry Moore, Salvador Dali, and Le Corbusier. "I have really always liked eclectic design, a combination of the contemporary and the antique," she says. "I grew up with beautiful old pieces, then I learned about totally contemporary design. Now I have both."

Above: Atrium space, Commerzbank, Paris, France, a project done by Owen & Mandolfo in conjunction with the architecture firm Beraud + Berbesson. Photograph by Deide von Schaewen.

A selection of Owen's work appears on pages 152 to 155.

LUCA VIGNELLI

Lella **Vignelli**

Above: Artemide lighting showroom, International Design Center, New York City. Photograph by Antonia Mulas.

F or any architect or designer visiting New York City, the journey to Tenth Avenue and 36th Street is a pilgrimage on par with visiting Lourdes. On the penthouse floor of a warehouse building is the headquarters of Vignelli Associates, a space completed and occupied in 1986 that is still winning design awards well into the 1990s. One enters the 15,000-square-foot space through massive double doors surfaced with hand-waxed lead. There follows a fifty-foot-long processional, with walls of silvery gridded aluminum, culminating in a guest-seating arrangement under dramatic windows, which present the landscape of Manhattan and the Hudson River. Even the floor underfoot reinforces the Vignelli signature for innovation: it is a hard, gray composite surface often used in garages.

Lella Vignelli, executive vice-president of Vignelli Associates and president of Vignelli Designs, the product and furniture arm of the firm, works in an office off the seating area, composed of a sitting room with a sofa and circular dining/conference table, and a work space with a square desk surrounded by four chairs. The walls, as in the rest of the executive offices, are gridded in blonde particle board, stained white, and lacquered—but used like fine wood. All upholstery is black. In the white, light-filled studio behind this space, where as many as thirty staff work on the boards, one wall is constructed of corrugated galvanized steel. All the workstations are made of inexpensive sheetrock.

The reductive minimalism reiterating a geometry in monotones does not describe the Vignelli polemic completely. Vignelli emphasizes that she and her partner, husband Massimo Vignelli, have always tried to make "poor materials work for us in an elegant way." In the 1960s a vocabulary of industrial carpet, white walls, and restaurant-table bases with plain Formica© laminate tops described their philosophy. In what Vignelli declares are the "austerity nineties," there is a new lexicon of particle board, galvanized metal, industrial tubes, composite flooring, and aluminum sheets, but the goal is the same: to explore ordinary materials with extraordinary applications. "We have never embraced an obsolete point of view," says Vignelli. "We are not interested in fashion and style. We completely avoided the Postmodernist style with its exotic woods, inlaid decorations, and baroque richness. It lasted only five to ten years and now it is gone." She notes that the same fate befell the Memphis era at the beginning of the 1980s and adds, "We are against trends. They may be important culturally, but professionally I find they are unethical, and they generally cost more to build than a straight design because they are not going to last."

Born in Udine in northern Italy, Vignelli came to the United States on a tuition fellowship as a special student at the Massachusetts Institute of Technology School of Architecture in 1958. A year later she joined the Chicago office of Skidmore Owings & Merrill as a junior designer. In 1960, returning to Italy, she established the Vignelli Office of Design and Architecture in Milan with Massimo Vignelli. She became a registered architect in 1962, although in Europe the boundaries of an architect's provenance are more blurred than they are in the United States. Vignelli exerts her design skills comfortably in many scales, from tableware, vases, and accessories to furniture, both residential and commercial, and interior architecture and design, including showrooms, exhibition spaces, offices, museums, galleries, and residences.

For the past twenty-five years she has worked in the United States, first as head of the interior department for Unimark International Corporation, and then (since 1971) as a principal of her own firm. In this time span, the Vignelli touch and search for excellence have been employed by more than twenty-five product manufacturers (including Knoll International, Sasaki, Corning Glass, Formica Corporation, Stendig International, and Bernhardt Contract) and about fifty major corporations (from Xerox to Olivetti, Jaguar, and Fiat).

The firm has also received attention from the media and from numerous museums. It has been the subject of two feature-length television programs that have been broadcast worldwide. The Vignellis were the first designers to be invited to exhibit in the former Soviet Union, following the proclamation of glasnost in 1988. Lella Vignelli's designs—strong, stark, and pure in their aesthetics—are in the permanent collections of The Museum of Modern Art, the Cooper-Hewitt Museum, and The Metropolitan Museum of Art in New York, as well as the Musée des Arts Decoratifs in Montreal and Die Neue Sammlung in Munich. They have won her recognition from the AIA, with the Gold Medal award for Industrial Arts, and membership in the *Interior Design* Hall of Fame.

Still, it is more than mere forms and materials, objects and their arrangement in spaces, that draw pilgrims to the penthouse on Tenth Avenue. It is the beacon for the future, informing the design community of the way ahead. In an uncertain world, who does not want to know what's next? The Vignellis made a critical statement in moving their office from a conventional midtown address in the East 60s to a location that was seen as an industrial wasteland of undesirable character. Yet within no time, they had proved that trading Park Avenue status for more generous space and low overhead made sense in a time of rapidly shifting social and cultural values. Never known for wavering or sitting on the fence, always setting the pace with an innate sense of clairvoyance, Lella Vignelli is convinced

Above: Saratoga furniture line, manufactured by Poltronova, designed by Vignelli. Photograph by Aldo Ballo.

Above: Silver altar objects designed for New York's Saint Peter's Church. Photograph by George Cserna.

that global thinking must be everyone's objective: "Our firm today has the capacity to turn out work in six different languages directly from New York, including Japanese. Languages are vital now if you want to work in product design because there are so few American manufacturers left. But it's not only the language that has to be understood in order to work in other countries. We must master things like the metric system, as well as cultural differences."

The Vignellis are not establishing satellite offices overseas or joint-venture operations but prefer to do an entire job directly from New York, providing all the working drawings in the language and format required by the particular location and country. "Fax has changed everything, even the way we present our ideas to clients," notes Vignelli. "Before we used to show big blueprints; now we show smaller drawings in a booklet form, which can be easily faxed." In terms of personal communications, Vignelli spends about one or two weeks out of every five traveling to see clients, anywhere in the world.

Economics is also driving a new sensibility in design, Vignelli says: "It took a year to go from a mentality of affluence to one of austerity, and it all happened in 1990. We don't believe that the type of affluence seen in the 1980s will ever come back, so as designers we have to start working in a different way. We feel quite comfortable in it, we have always given lasting values, and this will be the spirit of the nineties. I believe we are retreating to ethical values of the fifties and sixties. The game is not to try to impress people by being trendy but to be more true to yourself. The concept of piling on more and more will have to change, to one of creating more with less."

Since the majority of cultural and social changes have historically begun with economics, Vignelli expects the 1990s to be a decade of "new twists on many things." And New York, she predicts, will be the primary stage because it contains the most creative energy in the world. "The ends of centuries are not marked by dates but by historical events," she remarks. "The nineteenth century was defined by the wars of 1805 and 1914. The twentieth century dates from 1914 and ends in 1989 with the freedom revolutions in the Communist countries of the Eastern bloc. We don't need to wait for the year 2000 to see what is going to happen in the next century or the next millennium. We are changing now. These will be great times."

A selection of Vignelli's work appears on pages 156 to 159.

Opposite, top: In the Manhattan offices of Bonnie Lunt, an advertising executive search firm, 200-year-old barn siding is juxtaposed against glass brick in the conference room. The Clodagh-designed table top, of Pennsylvania blue stone inlaid with aluminum strips, is poised atop a custom terra-cotta base by Bennett Bean. Vernacular-style aluminum office chairs surround the table. Photograph by Daniel Aubry.

Opposite, bottom left: The steel entry door that leads to the reception area of the Lunt office was fabricated by Padhraic O'Cionna. A minimalist industrial effect pervades the space, augmented with steel tractor seats and steel tube-section vases. Photograph by Daniel Aubry.

Opposite, bottom right: In the Lunt project, a cantilevered reception desk, made of Pennsylvania blue stone, is paired with a corrugated aluminum chair by Mark Schaffer. Clodagh often commissions artists and craftspeople to create custom pieces for her installations. Photograph by Daniel Aubry.

Above: Clodagh's distinctive design vocabulary sweeps into the executive offices of a major corporation, the American Can Company in New York City, where granite floors and Zolatoned walls create a serene reception area environment. The seating with hide upholstery was designed by Clodagh and art furniture maker James Hong. Photograph by Peter Paige.

Above: Within the pared-down architectural envelope of this dining room in the Harrison residence, Manhattan, early nineteenth-century antique furniture and objects are combined with a purple slate and rusted steel table designed by Clodagh. The result is a striking, gallery-like environment where the emphasis is on the strength of individual forms. Photograph by Daniel Aubry.

Left: This patinated door in the Harrison residence is embellished with a custom-designed copper handle made by David Johnson. Photograph by Oberto Gili.

Opposite: In a New York City residence, Clodagh proclaims her masterly understanding of scale. The view from the dining area into the living room affords a glimpse of the varied forms and textures the designer is known for. Amusing touches, such as a monkey chair, are typical Clodagh touches. The concrete-and-wire bowl was designed by Jerry Kott. Photograph by Lizzie Himmel.

Above: To match the exuberant
personality of Steven Ross, the
company's Chief Executive Officer,
the reception area at Warner
Communications in New York City
is a lavishly detailed circular space
that involved two years of design
and construction. Elegantly placed
inside the perimeter of the gently
domed ceiling are light coves that
wash illumination across the curved
ceiling surface. A richly patterned
parquet floor band surrounds a
custom-fabricated carpet, upon
which are grouped classic lounge
chairs and antique side tables.
Photograph by Peter Aaron/Esto.

Opposite: The pharmaceutical giant
Schering-Plough inhabits 100,000
square feet of office space in Liberty
Corner, New Jersey. Groh's team
won the job by presenting the firm
with a new image of sleek moderni-
ty, exemplified by this reception
area. The gridded etched glass
wall and comfortable leather-
upholstered lounge chairs convey
the thoroughly contemporary, and
yet warm and comfortable, atmosphere desired by the client. Photograph by Durston Saylor.

Top: An elegantly curved stairway, rendered in hammered limestone with black ebonized wood detailing. connects three floors of the J. P. Stevens Company headquarters in New York City. Photograph by Durston Saylor.

Above: The CEO's suite at the WEA division of Time-Warner, New York City, is suggestive of the division's cutting-edge product line: records, tapes, and compact discs. A window

banquette, circular meeting table, and fluidly lined modern chairs respond to an executive whose preferred business style is informal. Photograph by Durston Saylor.

Left: In a temporary showroom for J. P. Stevens, the textile and home-furnishings manufacturer, Groh's design concept conveys a scenario for loft living to showcase the firm's Eileen West bed linen line. Photograph by Durston Saylor.

Above: The Cullinane designer dress shop at Phipps Plaza shopping center in Atlanta, Georgia, is a prototype retail store for a designer line of fashions and home furnishings. The space was conceived as a free-standing cabinet. The configuration in the shopping mall allowed for a gallery-like presentation, with all the store's merchandise visible from the pedestrian walkway. Suspended trelliswork conceals lighting and mechanical elements. Dressing rooms are suspended tents of translucent silk drapery. Project architect: Marti Cowan. Photograph by Steven Traves.

Left: The Adlersberg residence in Manhattan is a one-bedroom space built to accommodate the owner's specific requirements for home entertainment, work, and exercise. The cherrywood and steel-detailed dining table, designed by Helfand, separates in half to accommodate a parallelogram-shaped center leaf, allowing for flexible activity in the room. The bent-steel side chairs are also a Helfand design. The translucent door at left slides open to the kitchen area. Project architect: Marti Cowan. Photograph by Paul Warchol.

Opposite: Tension cables of braided bronze rope crisscross around the perimeter of Buffalo, a clothing store in Santa Monica, California. The ropes, which are used to display hanging garments, are anchored on exposed steel brackets. Folded clothing is displayed on cherrywood islands topped with panes of glass. Project architect: Marti Cowan. Photograph by Paul Warchol.

Opposite: The Jennifer Reed women's sportswear showroom in New York's garment district was designed in response to the company's eagerness to express its progressive design philosophy and commitment to the use of natural fibers in its products. The plan is liberated from the humdrum regularity of conventional geometry. Sculptural forms in cherrywood and ground steel and layered panes of glass coalesce into a decidedly modern vision. Project architect: Paul Rosenblatt. Photograph by Paul Warchol.

Above: The conference room and principal's office at Margaret Helfand Architects, in a brownstone in the Murray Hill section of New York City, acts as the firm's calling card. Chairs and tables, designed by Helfand in her idiosyncratic style, appear all the more provocative within the Victorian-style parlor floor dining-room space. Project architect: Marti Cowan. Photograph by Paul Warchol.

Right: In the entrance vestibule of the Helfand office, the combination of varied materials signals the designer's preoccupation with experimentation. Wood composite boards are used for the shelving. The flooring is a rubber-tire derivative. Photograph by Paul Warchol.

Above: A rigorous sense of symmetry is evident in an executive dining room at the Merrill Lynch headquarters in New York's World Financial Center at Battery Park City. To give the space a residential feeling without its looking "decorated," the windows are fitted with wooden shutters. Photograph by Wolfgang Hoyt.

Above: A sparely railed stairway at the Citicorp offices in New York City represents the essence of minimalism. Iu had the wooden workstation/reception desk custom fabricated for the project. Photograph by Robert Miller.

*Above: The offices of the
Manufacturers Hanover Trust
Corporation in Los Angeles serve
as the company's center for trans-
Pacific leasing deals. The interiors
convey a sense of Asian serenity
and landscape through the use of
murals, plants, and light-colored
lacquered wood furnishings. Photograph by Paul Bielenberg.*

*Opposite: Upgrading a lobby space
is a common request of building
owners and developers in the 1990s.
Iu's simple and elegant renovation
of the One Liberty Plaza lobby in
New York City is a rigorous composition in white marble—used to
add a sense of increased height in
the space—with brushed stainless
steel panels, bronze accents, and
gold-leafed ceilings. Photograph
by Nathaniel Lieberman.*

Above: In Mallis's replanning of the lobby of the Becton Dickinson headquarters, Franklin Lakes, New Jersey, a grid pattern in the custom-designed carpeting is repeated in the richly detailed and curved wood reception desk. Photograph by Peter Aaron/Esto.

Left: Mallis's design for the VIP suite at Boston's Hynes Convention Center offers wood paneling and a traditional hearth as a focus, bringing a sense of stateliness to the space. Photograph by Peter Vanderwarker.

Opposite: The design program for the pub and galley of the Harvard Business School in Cambridge, Massachusetts, called for a collegiate ambience. Mallis chose not to replicate the traditional Georgian campus style, instead selecting contemporary furnishings and fixtures that give the interiors a club-like feeling. The carpeting was dyed to match the crimson associated with the university and the oak paneling was custom stained in a rich reddish tone. Photograph by Steve Rosenthal.

Above: A refurbishing of this classroom at the Groton School, Groton, Massachusetts, part of the preparatory academy's Schoolhouse Renovation and Addition Project, involved restoration of its traditional configuration and furnishings. The yellow pine floor was refinished. The existing instructor's desk and student tablet-arm seating were also refinished. Several new wood chairs, made to match the existing stock, were crafted for the project by prisoners in the Massachusetts Correctional Institution, under Mallis's supervision. Photograph by Doug Cooke, Dillon Photography.

Above: The corporate headquarters of Milco Industries in New York City incorporates a workroom where samples of women's lingerie are made. The building structure was exposed throughout, and spaces rigorously planned along the perimeter for the maximum influx of natural light. Photograph by Wolfgang Hoyt.

Above: America, a restaurant in New York City's Flatiron District, embraces the "dining as theater" concept. The space, formerly the street floor of a nineteenth-century department store, features furnishings and decorations of traditional American origin. Photograph by Mark Darley.

Opposite: Within the restored beaux-arts splendor of Washington, D.C.'s Union Station is a 17,000-square-foot branch of the restaurant America. The murals that cover wall surfaces depict American heroes and landscapes, playing up the optimism associated with the era when the railroads were built. Photograph by Masao Ueda.

Above: Located at the South Street Seaport in lower Manhattan, this restaurant, the Liberty Café, in the waterfront mall was designed around a maritime theme. Murals incorporating maps and waterway scenes, sculptured plaster sea gulls overhead, and a chugging locomotive around the bar connote the spirit of exploration. Glass-globed, flame-form torchères provide a festive decorative touch. Photograph by Mark Darley.

Opposite: The client's design directive for the Café Greco was simple: create a lighthearted bistro with the character of a space in a traditional Mediterranean hill town in a former New York City tenement building. Café tables and woven wicker chairs help to create the atmosphere, as does a specially executed bacchanalian scene painted above the bar. Photograph by Masao Ueda.

Above: The living room in Owen's Greek revival-style weekend house in New York's Hudson Valley offers a sense of rustic simplicity with modern influences. Original details were preserved and beautiful old wood window frames and moldings were exposed. Photograph by Billy Cunningham.

Opposite: A Houston, Texas, residence, designed during Owen's tenure at Innerplan, was conceived as a background for a museum-quality collection of modern art. The sparely furnished dining room offers cool travertine floors and classic modern furniture pieces. The painting is by Kenneth Noland. Photograph by Jaime Ardiles-Arce.

Above: Davidoff of Geneva, a men's tobacco and accessories store on Rodeo Drive in Beverly Hills, is the first of a prototype store design to be implemented by the firm world wide. Pearwood paneled walls are paired with a limestone floor, giving a sophisticated, contemporary image to the space, with appeal to both male and female customers. Owen & Mandolfo, Inc; senior designer: Lawrence E. Charity. Photograph by Toshi Yoshimi.

Left: The Manhattan headquarters of Commerzbank, located on three floors of the World Financial Center, amount to 130,000 square feet. This chief executive's suite, with a commanding view of New York Harbor, was designed as a classically contemporary business setting, with clean-lined furnishings and custom mill work. Owen & Mandolfo, Inc; senior designer: Anthony Mandolfo. Photograph by Peter Paige.

Opposite: The dual-level Charles Jourdan footwear and fashion shop, in New York City's Trump Tower, is a symphony of grids: a gridded ceiling incorporates lighting and security systems; an etched-glass screen shields an escalator. The comfortable lounge seating is slipcovered in leather. The project was completed by Owen while a partner at the Innerplan firm. Senior designer: Anthony Mandolfo. Photograph by Jaime Ardiles-Arce.

Above: A series of columns, made of cold-rolled steel, organize the draped display spaces in the pared-down showroom design for Poltrona Frau, an Italian furnishings manufacturer, at the International Design Center, New York (IDCNY). Photograph by Antonia Mulas.

Above: In the showroom the Vignelli office designed for Artemide, a lighting company, at the IDCNY, a sleek rawness pervades the space. Product display is reduced to the minimum—a Vignelli-designed table and a freestanding flight of stairs—in the series of rooms that lead into one another. Photograph by Antonia Mulas.

Right: Within the offices of Vignelli Associates, located in an industrial building on Manhattan's West Side, a formal symmetry is created from space to space. Photograph by Mario Carrieri.

Above: In the Poltrona Frau showroom, at the firm's headquarters
in Tolentino, Italy, furniture is
treated like sculpture. Products,
such as the Vignelli–designed CEO
executive furniture line on display,
are the focus of attention in the
gallery-like spaces. Photograph by
Antonia Mulas.

Opposite: With the interior of Saint
Peter's Church, located at the foot
of the Citicorp tower in midtown
Manhattan, Vignelli created a new
standard for modern ecclesiastical
interiors. All the components—
pews, kneelers, altar appointments,
pulpit, and font—were refined to
a minimal expression of form.
Photograph by George Cserna.

Pamela **Babey**

POETS

Like fine artists, Poets are unpredictable and

seem to break all the rules, while they create new

standards for the future. They stretch their

imaginations in all directions and are likely to

focus on several levels simultaneously, applying

their talents in fields other than interior design.

These artist-practitioners share a passion for

detail and for innovation in the design

of the interior landscape.

Pamela Babey's desk is littered with eccentric memora-bilia—a collection of tassels that she considers one of her hallmarks, a dozen swatches of her current favorite textiles, construction models, toy airplanes from her countless trips around the world, and even significant messages from fortune cookies. A massive glass vase, filled with fresh-cut flowers, is always present, giving the work space a powerful perfume. The overall ambience is tantalizing and seductive, and it embodies the work of a woman whose clients stretch from Singapore and Hong Kong to London, Paris, Brussels, and Milan, with many stops in between. She is president of Babey Moulton in San Francisco, a firm she founded in 1991 after the death of designer Charles Pfister, with whom she had collabo-rated for ten years.

The femininity evident in the loft office space belies a strong interest in the nuts and bolts—the functional aspects—of design and architecture, as much as it embraces an almost fanatical attraction to beauty, particularly in textures and col-ors. Babey knew from her early school days in Las Cruces, New Mexico, where her family moved from Brooklyn, New York, when she was a child, that she was destined for a career in design. She leaned toward civil engineering but was persuaded to study architecture ("Engineering was considered far too much an all-male field for a woman to be successful," she ex-plains) and obtained a bachelor's degree at the University of California, Berkeley, in 1968.

While working at the New York office of Skidmore Owings & Merrill, her first employer, Babey realized that inte-rior design was going to be her specialty. Her inquiring eye was developed by the legendary associate partner in charge of inte-rior design, Davis Allen, and through his tutelage she discov-ered the world of eclecticism. Babey notes, "Up to that point I was schooled in strict Modernism, but Dave opened doors. He lived in an apartment that was far from the SOM style—a mix of this and that, found pieces, not the common Mies and Breuer chairs. He showed me that many things can come together suc-cessfully in an interior. It was a revelation, and I loved this ex-posure." The learning experience with Allen continued on a number of projects.

Back in San Francisco in the early seventies she met the

designer who was to be her most important influence after Allen: Pfister. He hired her to work with him in the SOM office there. Pfister was given to extraordinary flights of imagination: a wall covered with a diamond-shaped lattice of shelving, each of the myriad alcoves filled with a crystal vase containing a single orchid, was typical of the many ideas he would dream up in a day. Pfister thought big and lavishly, but with a remarkable sense of refinement and detail. Babey soaked up his intuitive, gut-reaction method of problem solving. "Charles just had to do something because it felt right, no matter what the circumstance or the budget," Babey reflects. "It was exhilarating."

In 1981, when Pfister decided to open his own San Francisco office, he asked Babey to join him. She held out for a special relationship. The request was not just for a title—she has always found titles to be "repulsive"—but total control, with Pfister, over the development of all the work coming out of the office. Pfister had no hesitation in meeting her demand, and they launched the firm with just two other employees—a secretary and a project manager, Joseph Matzo.

Over the next nine years, until Pfister's untimely death at the age of fifty in 1990, the two designers established a symbiotic relationship, designing on the backs of envelopes while in airplanes, faxing back design ideas to the ever-growing team in San Francisco, meeting clients across the globe. The fusion of their personalities resulted in a series of outstanding design solutions for their roster of blue-chip clients, including Deutsche Bank, Shell, and American billionaire Marshall Cogan.

Since Babey established her own firm with her three partners from the Pfister office, David Moulton, Michael Booth, and Gerald Giu, her personal signature can be seen across a broad range of work: in the new Trinity Properties headquarters in San Francisco, the new showroom for The Knoll Group in Brussels, the refurbished Park Hyatt Hotel in Chicago, the new Regent Hotel in Milan, and two important residences (whose owners, because of their prominence, must remain nameless).

There is a precision to Babey's creativity that clients clearly admire, a search for a modern adaptation of the authentic, which characterizes every job. For example, elaborate grillework doors and screens were developed for the Hotel Las Fuentes in Pasadena, along with massive wrought-iron chandeliers, each with fifty glass lamp shades custom-made in Venice, to evoke the indigenous flavor of the California Mission style. In the recently completed Regent Hotel in Milan, a complex renovation of a fourteenth-century monastery, fresco-like dadoes were designed as cornices for each room. While many Modernist-trained architects love to cut a swathe of pure twentieth century through whatever they do, Babey will stop and think about what is appropriate—not only for the location, the site, and the neighborhood, but for the client, whose character and inclinations must also be expressed.

Given her own preferences, every interior would be done exclusively in camel, black, and white, which she considers the consummate background colors for the eclectic gathering of furnishings and objects with which she likes to personalize a space. But played out over this basic scheme will be a layering of textures and materials. She describes the thought process as similar to that involved in creating theater sets, or in fashion design, where layer is placed over layer, for a totality of texture and harmony.

It is with textiles that Babey has an unerring sense of the "perfect" choice and an affinity that she candidly admits is almost an addiction. She will journey to the Ratti mill in northern Italy perhaps half a dozen times a year, to work with the weavers on custom-dyed paisleys, which she selects not only for her residential clients but also for commercial clients who have the taste and bravura to follow her inclinations. Within the last year, her touch with textiles has resulted in the production of a personal collection, the end product of five years of extensive and intensive research to produce the quality and the refinement that is quintessentially Pamela Babey: an assortment of silks and damasks, weaves and textures of breathtaking beauty and sensuality.

Top: "Ratti and Paisley" textile exhibit design, Fashion Institute of Technology, New York. Photograph by Dale Wing.

Above: "In Flight" carpet design for V'Soske and materials relating to its realization. Photograph by Phil Toy.

A selection of Babey's work appears on pages 176 to 181.

LARRY BARNS

Gretchen
Bellinger

In the 1980s design entrepreneur Gretchen Bellinger could be found in all the predictable locations in New York City. She had a spacious showroom for her textile collections at the Decoration & Design building on Third Avenue, her offices and warehouse were on East 59th Street, and she lived nearby on 57th Street, in a high-style apartment that confirmed her reputation as one of the leading influences in the world of design. But in 1989 everything changed. Almost overnight, she decentralized—in a textbook example of *Megatrends* author John Naisbitt's forecast that farsighted entrepreneurs and businesses would pull out of major metropolitan centers for economic and psychological reasons, choosing instead to operate in smaller-scale environments.

Today Gretchen Bellinger Inc is firmly established 150 miles north of Manhattan in the town of Cohoes, a suburb of Albany, the capital of New York State, in a red-brick warehouse building overlooking the confluence of the Mohawk and Hudson rivers. She has the luxury of space, the aesthetic pleasure of generous windows and refinished oak floors, and the total absence of big-city frustrations. "There's more peace to get on with work, and life is more civilized. There's not so much rush," she affirms, over a poached salmon and strawberries lunch in her conference space. "It's hard to understand why I didn't do it earlier." She is only two hours from her favorite refuge, Camp Bellinger, on the shores of Long Lake in the Adirondacks. There, a rustic house, which she uses frequently for both business and private entertaining, exemplifies her singular touch in interior design. The entire house is done in shades of taupe and beige, with Bellinger cotton on banquettes, Bellinger silks for lampshades and bedspreads, even Bellinger canvas for the deck chairs on the boat dock. For day-to-day living, the Manhattan apartment has been replaced by a gracious Victorian farmhouse on several acres, only fifteen minutes' drive from the office.

While only two of her thirty staff chose to move with her from Manhattan, Bellinger found no problem in regrouping and indeed proved that restructuring added stability to her business. In New York, high-quality personnel were difficult to find and hard to keep. They also tended to use the office as an extension of their social lives, tying up telephones with personal calls and gossiping about numerous non-work-related activities. In Cohoes, the staff is family-oriented and goes home at night. The office is truly a place for work.

Bellinger was not educated as an interior designer, yet she is without question a force in the industry, simply because her ideas and fabrics find their way into the most prestigious projects, from the color scheme of the supersonic Concorde to the guest rooms of Four Seasons hotels, top banks, law offices, and the residences of the rich and famous. Graduating from Cranbrook Academy as a weaver, she first joined Skidmore Owings & Merrill's Chicago office in 1970, as a librarian in charge of resources. "The office was in its heyday, and I worked in a beehive of excitement," recalls Bellinger. Legendary architects Walter Netsch, Bruce Graham, and Myron Goldsmith

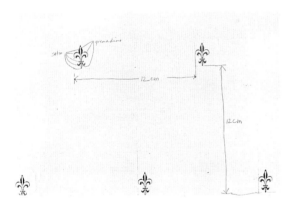

Top: Working sketch for Fleur de Lis tissue taffeta fabric.

Above: Fleur de Lis tissue taffeta, a Bellinger fabric offered in three colors. Photograph by Paul Pearl.

were partners. Donald Powell, Robert Kleinschmidt, Margaret McCurry, George Larson, Patrick McConnell, Klaus Müller, Steven Ronson, and Nava Andric were junior designers. It was Bellinger's job to help them choose materials—tiles, textiles, lighting, marbles, hardware, ceiling finishes, carpets, laminates, and plumbing fixtures—for their projects. She caught on to the SOM aesthetic, right down to the flower arrangements that she chose for the partners' offices every Monday morning, and SOM appreciated her taste. "I saw that the firm had a total commitment to design. How they kept up their offices was as important as the way they presented work to clients or designed a building. It influenced me and still does today," she says, alluding to the regimented taupe pencil containers on each of her employees' desks, filled with immaculately sharpened taupe-colored pencils—a color that has become a Bellinger hallmark.

With a talent for organization, Bellinger set about improving the way the SOM library was set up, helping to develop it into a specially designed room, with installations of different lighting fixtures, so that materials could be viewed under varying conditions. Her close connection with fabrics and textiles led her to observe a gap in the market. With the oncoming boom in commercial design—hotels, restaurants, corporate offices, museums, and other large facilities—it was clear that new and more appropriate products were necessary. SOM architects and designers did not want to furnish the interiors of their glass skyscrapers with flowered chintzes and satin damasks. They preferred more tailored fabrics, but there were few on the market, and those that were available were unimaginative.

By 1975, after brief stints creating textile collections at Knoll, V'Soske, and Donghia in New York City, she established her own fabric company, based in her apartment, with a first collection of thirteen "restyled classic" fabrics, including the Limousine Cloth and Pullman Cloth that are still in the line today. All were made from natural fibers—cotton, wool, and silk—which, she recalls, was "a radical idea in 1976, when synthetics were fashionable." She identified twenty design firms to whom she wanted to sell, wrapped small fabric swatches over pieces of cardboard, and placed them in elegantly embossed boxes. It was a marketing "first." Her imaginative effort pulled in the clients, and the sophisticated fabrics for commercial applications hit the mark.

Soon there were more "firsts." A personalized advertising campaign, showing Bellinger atop a pile of pillows covered in mouth-watering colored fabrics, helped to position the company. "It was controversial and I was aware of the gossip, but I was the only woman out there and a natural target," she points out. "I'm not going to say that it still isn't tough today. People still think of women as a minority, and I am happy to take advantage of the opportunities for women in business, but we forget that women are the majority of the population in this country. The facts don't seem to relate to the reality." Bellinger adds that she could describe innumerable business situations in which men have lined up together, whether or not they liked one another, just to demonstrate gender solidarity. "Women

have yet to reach this level of cooperation," she comments, "and we lose out."

Despite the numerous challenges she encountered during fifteen years in business, Bellinger soldiered on, continuing to bring out outstanding, award-winning products. Isadora was the first pleated silk to be offered to the commercial design market; Diva was a breakthrough in stylized decorative fabrics, with its rhinestone appliqués on silk—it even found its way into the United Kingdom headquarters of Morgan Stanley. Architectural Screen was a sensational steel–mesh fabric, now off the market because bootleggers went directly to her source for the material. (The knock-offs of this particular "fabric" are not quite as effective as Bellinger's version—her competitors didn't understand that Bellinger had applied a special finish to the material.)

As the creative spirit bubbled year after year, Bellinger also accrued an astonishing number of trademarked and registered fabrics. To date, almost one hundred original designs have been listed: seventy-nine trademarked, ten registered, two registered collections, and four trademarked collections. Yachting Cotton, Skimmer linen (with colors named after birds), Casting Illusions (named after fishing lures), Camp plaids, and Prima Donna Lurex on silk were some that defined the range of her inventions, from basic to opulent. Ninety-five percent of the apt names for the textiles were her own inventions. In tune with the environmental sensibilities in the air, she progressed to more figurative concepts, introducing a trademarked "Stars, B's, and Fleur de Lis" collection which demonstrated that she could be decorative without losing her signature tailored quality. And a reinvestigation of synthetics such as polyester, seen in one of her newest collections, "Dot...to...Dot," has broadened the line beyond natural fibers.

Bellinger takes an equally creative approach to management, refusing to be dragooned into conventional attitudes, although her business tycoon/chemical engineer father has always been a role model. "I believe that you have to jump into business, rather like learning to swim. You can theorize all you like about strokes on dry land, but only by getting in the water can you put it all together and find out if you can do it."

A selection of Bellinger's work appears on pages 182 to 187.

ELIZABETH LEHMANN

Patricia Conway

The mezzanine restaurant overlooking the famous gold-leafed stairway at the Paramount Hotel in New York City is perhaps the ideal place for Patricia Conway, dean of the Graduate School of Fine Arts at the University of Pennsylvania, to make her point. It is that for the past decade the most memorable interior design projects, those that have caught national attention, have been executed by someone other than a dedicated commercial interior designer: an architect, sculptor, painter, graphic designer, or decorator. The two designers who worked on New York's Paramount Hotel exemplify this trend. Philippe Starck is an artist with no formal training in architecture or decorative arts who is busy building structures in Japan and designing everything from hotels to toothbrushes! Paul Haigh is a British-born jack-of-all-trades who graduated from the Royal College of Art in London. Conway herself is in the vortex of debate about credentials in the interior design field. She is neither an architect, artist, nor interior designer by training, but she now holds an impressive academic post and just recently relinquished her responsibilities as CEO of the firm Kohn Pedersen Fox Conway, winner of *Interiors* magazine's Designer of the Year award in 1987. Her education is in English literature and planning, and it is the latter area of expertise (she holds a master's degree from Columbia University School of Architecture) that has propelled her career.

Conway has witnessed the rise of commercial interior design since she joined the firm of John Carl Warnecke as the associate planning director in 1974, and its evolution into the big time, a far cry from an activity engaged in by the stereotypical lady decorators in hats. It was at Warnecke, while involved in the interior design projects on the boards, that she met her three future partners—Eugene Kohn, William Pedersen, and Shelley Fox—with whom, in the depths of the 1976 recession, she set up an independent operation. (They hired a secretary but made a commitment to take no pay for themselves for the first six months.)

Almost immediately the group discovered that Conway's particular area of expertise was a plus on their calling card. "Planning is the direct opposite of architecture," notes Conway. "It is about the synthesis of ideas, not about the analytical process, but it is a tremendous enhancement to architecture. It's a tool in the design process. We quickly found that when we did a presentation we made magic, because our personalities, our intellects, and our abilities were complementary. So we made a very powerful quartet."

In fact, almost twenty years after KPF set up shop, the AIA reported in a roundtable study that the "predesign," or planning, phase of a project typically added 10 to 15 percent to the charge for normal services, and that quality came from concentrating on this first phase. Ironically, many architecture firms still do not offer a planning service but rely on outside consultants to do this job—and thus miss out on being fully involved in a strategically vital part of the project, not to mention the fees. And it is with this understanding that the most respected interior design firms have found their footing and

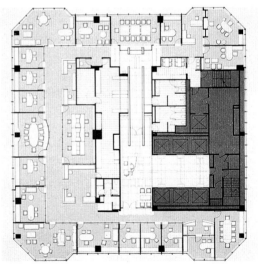

Above: Floor plan, offices for a private investment firm, New York City.

carved out a newly defined role and discipline, which is now being recognized by major clients. In 1984 Conway and partners saw the wisdom of setting up a separate entity, Kohn Pedersen Fox Conway, to allow their fully integrated interior design business to flourish. Typically, 85 percent of the firm's work was commissioned for buildings other than those designed by Kohn Pedersen Fox.

Conway remarks, "To me, planning is of more overriding and compelling concern than any other process, and it has been the secret of my personal success, because I have been able to straddle the professions of architecture and interior design. There are very few professionals in either discipline cross-trained in planning, so I am unique. There is no precedent. In other words, I am a fluke."

Before accepting her current academic post, Conway often carried eight different jobs at once at KPFC, working with the client (usually at the level of chairman of the board or president) at the front end, on buildings, leases, work letters, budgeting, scope, and long-term strategy. KPFC's roster of blue-chip clients included Ameritrust, NCNB, CBS, The Rockefeller Foundation, Viacom, Capital Cities/ABC, MONY, Financial Services, the Equitable Life Assurance Society, Proctor & Gamble, General Mills, HBO, AT&T, and Bear Stearns. The firm also designed hotel interiors, art galleries, and residences. Conway's extraordinarily heavy work load was more often than not augmented by "side" activities: writing the books *Ornamentalism: The New Decorativeness in Architecture and Design* (Clarkson N. Potter, 1983) and *Art for Everyday: The New Craft Movement* (Potter, 1990), extramural education (she won a Loeb Fellowship at the Harvard Graduate School of Design in 1986), and civic and professional responsibilities (as a board member of the International Design Conference at Aspen, the Parks Council in New York City, and the St. Ann Center for Restoration and the Arts in Brooklyn).

Writing was almost a vocation for Conway (she worked as a design journalist before taking up planning), and her skills in this area enabled her to express her firm's evolving design philosophies. *Ornamentalism*, still selling nearly ten years after publication, was one of the first books to codify Postmodernism—the trend toward historicism and decoration that occurred from 1970 onwards—a style that was emblematic of KPF. *Art for Everyday* showcased the contemporary talent in the American craft movement and demonstrated how artisans were brought into the design process by KPFC, in both commercial and residential spaces. The firm believed in cooperation with such artisans at the start of a project and always employed textile specialists on its staff.

Indeed, it was this effort to introduce one-of-a-kind artifacts—a specially designed wood, marble, or metal-inlaid floor, carpet, piece of furniture, light fixture, or textile—that helped KPFC establish a unique image in interior design and win numerous design awards. For the prestigious *Interiors* award, a portfolio of work was shown that was breathtaking in its richness and decoration. A custom-made boardroom table for the

Equitable Life Assurance Company, of mahogany and walnut burl, seating more than fifty board members, was enriched with leather blotters, inlaid with bronze, and offered individual bronze reading lights. Fine mill work reinterpreting the Georgian style embellished the executive floors, meeting the Equitable chairman's request for a Jeffersonian "colonial" ambience. A fiftieth-floor dining room, with a forty-foot-high vaulted ceiling and arched windows swagged with crimson draperies, became the quintessential example of 1980s' boomtime opulence, a treatment that even filtered down to the general employee work floors, where office workstations were customized in the Georgian style. Moldings, entablatures, columns and capitals, chair rails, and parquet floors all evinced a strong reliance on craftspeople in the creative process.

Even when the opulent eighties gave way to the austere nineties, KPFC continued in its resolve to handcraft the interior environment—but corporate repositioning, in tune with shareholders' rejection of flamboyant luxury, led the firm to stress qualities of functionality and endurance, with less emphasis on baroque historicism.

As she views the next decade, Conway, swinging now toward academia, is positioning herself for more growth, which she considers vital to a satisfying career. Relying, as she always has, on intuition and gut reaction for her guides, she appears, once again, to be placing herself "in the right place at the right time." Education is now a "hot button." Conway sees two distinct interior design professions coexisting—one whose practitioners have interior design–based educations, from schools of home economics or fine-arts programs, and another consisting of individuals with architecture degrees who do interiors—and her goals are to initiate some curriculum consistency between the two, lead inquiries about the diverse standards current in the field, and pinpoint the shortfalls in the recently enacted legislation that ensures professional status for interior design.

Conway fully understands the reluctance of architects to accept interior design as a stand-alone discipline. It was one reason, she admits, for the establishment of KPFC in the first place—to remove the interior design business from the architectural milieu. She notes, "Any discussion of women in interior design must ask whether interior design is viewed by male architects as a second-class profession because it was traditionally practiced by women in an era when almost all architects were men, or whether the two-dimensional training of interior design does result in a lesser skill than that produced by the three-dimensional training and broader education of architects." She believes that if indeed there is such a culture gap, it must be understood—and closed. No doubt the new dean, with her executive capabilities, will soon start enacting the appropriate measures to get this done.

A selection of Conway's KPFC work appears on pages 188 to 193.

Frances **Halsband**

It is brunchtime in Woodstock, New York, the scene of the famous 1969 rock concert, and further back in time, the gatherings of people of arts and letters at the Woodstock Guild during the 1930s. Woodstock in the 1990s remains a gathering place for artists, and on this Saturday morning two creative women of stature—architect Frances Halsband and novelist Gail Godwin, both of whom have homes in the town— are meeting at a local restaurant to discuss the novelist's new book. Godwin is in search of authentic background information for the novel's protagonist, a woman architect.

She could not have chosen a better role model than Halsband. In 1985 she was elected the first woman president for a four-year term of the 101-year-old Architectural League of New York. In 1991 she assumed the presidency of the New York chapter of the AIA and was named dean of the School of Architecture at Pratt Institute, Brooklyn: two more "firsts" for a woman. Halsband sees the decade of the 1990s as a breakthrough era for architecture and design simply because it is the first time that a significant number of women are in leadership roles with a characteristic leadership style—"collaborative, creative, and innovative, working with groups, breaking down barriers between disciplines, combining things or people in new ways, joining and connecting people and ideas. The collaborative aspects of this leadership style are probably related to the characteristics of personality or culture that are traditionally women's attributes: nurturing, mothering, helping."

In conversation, Godwin identifies another trait that might also be attributed to a feminine attitude to life, which is evident in Halsband's personal approach to her career: paying attention to the matter at hand, as a result of which the next matters naturally appear. According to Godwin, an evolving pattern is a more natural way to proceed than a ladder pattern (conquering rung by rung until the top is reached), which may come to be seen as obsolete and destructive to the natural patterns of the human psyche. Perhaps for this reason, the idea of restoring and rehabilitating what is already there, "growing" a design project from its existing roots, is something that resonates strongly with Halsband, whether it's designing a traffic circle in Woodstock (which she planted with tulips and daffodils) or salvaging Manhattan subway stations to recover the sense of their past glory, the days when a five-cent ride bought

Above: Stairway, Computer Science Building, Princeton University. Photograph by Cervin Robinson.

a pleasant transportation experience, and stations were decorated with colorful and symbolic pictorial tiles.

With a high-school background in science and math, a love of the craft of drawing, and a 1960s' college experience involving peace marches and fervent dedication to social issues, Halsband approaches her profession with the conviction that it is more than just "art." She believes it concerns sensible use of the land, ecology, and civic responsibility—a complex roster of intimately connected issues. "You can no longer just dig a hole for the plumber and put a building down anywhere. We are not dealing with a closed system. There is no endless horizon. People have lost track of the fact that rain forests in South America and even carpet glue are connected to the big picture," she emphasizes. Equally important, in her opinion, is the user's experience of interior space, because the function of a building is not merely to be aesthetically pleasing on the outside but to provide functional, comfortable space on the inside.

A micro example of Halsband's all-inclusive mind-set is her own office, on the light-filled top floor of a midtown Manhattan warehouse building, the current headquarters of the firm she opened with her architect husband, Robert Kliment, in 1972. Two early nineteenth-century corner armchairs face a modern, streamlined desk. A seven-drawer Arts & Crafts chest is tucked into a recess, while at her drawing table, four plastic containers—pink, green, yellow, and purple—hold pens and magic markers.

Out in the studio, where about twenty employees are "on the boards," the juxtapositions continue. Models can be seen of the latest luxury house, with an immense entertaining room as big as many apartments, alongside a low-budget, *pro bono* solution for a Manhattan street newsstand and the design of a new entry for the Long Island Railroad terminal on West 34th Street. Framed photographs of published work speak to an intense interest in light and lighting, as well as furniture design that evokes aspects of the Arts & Crafts movement.

Principal interiors include offices for the law firm of McCarter & English, winner of the 1989 American Bar Association Design Award, the Alvin Ailey American Dance Theater Foundation, and offices for the Random House publishing company. Residential work includes everything from mega-size million-dollar homes to house additions, guest houses, and apartments. The interior design is always reflective of the architecture, never at odds with it, as so often happens when the latest fashionable decorating "look" takes over indiscriminately. Wherever a building is located, it embraces the site comfortably, with warmth and historical references, seeking the essence that ties together many elements. This sensitivity succeeded in winning the firm, among other projects, the job of rebuilding the town hall in Salisbury, Connecticut. (They were selected from a pool of twenty-seven architects invited to submit proposals.)

From the very beginning, Kliment and Halsband have designed all their own lighting fixtures—stepped-up alabaster glass sconces, inverted dome chandeliers, graceful pendant

Above: Residence on Martha's Vineyard. Photograph by Cervin Robinson.

lights of all shapes and sizes, recessed lighting that mixes various fixtures, comfortable desk lamps for reading and drawing, strategically positioned lamps for computer work, and torchères that throw uplighting to the ceiling from wrought-iron bases. These are designed along similar themes and variations, which Halsband relates to music (a calling she rejected at age sixteen because of its attendant isolation from the real world): "bigger, littler, softer, louder. I just keep refining the same ideas, as composers do." Also part of the Halsband signature is the use of wood, in stairways, interior walls, and furniture that has a sturdy, yet tactile, quality about it. It is this kind of interior detailing that leads design critics to describe the work as "rhapsodic," "different," and "neo-romantic."

When Louis I. Kahn was teaching at the University of Pennsylvania, encouraging his protégés to reach for metaphysical levels of space, Halsband caught the first whiff of excitement for her career path. "The architecture students *knew* they were going to change the world by the way they dealt with design," she says. "Studying literature, I felt helpless." When she began postgraduate studies in architecture at Columbia University, the first indication came that a competitive road lay ahead. Halsband recalls, "There were two women in the architecture class of thirty, and the professor told me in no uncertain terms that he resented the fact that we were taking up spaces in a class that could be used by men. He said we would never practice. As it happened, the other woman did get married and gave up. I carried on!" And noticeable today on the bookshelves in Halsband's office are the volumes of biographical reference books that place her name and achievements on an equal footing with those of men.

A selection of Halsband's work appears on pages 194 to 197.

ALAN WEINTRAUB

Lucia **Howard**

Above: Drafting room, Ace Architects offices, in the Leviathan, the firm's Oakland, California, headquarters building. Photograph by Alan Weintraub.

Approaching the Leviathan, the headquarters of Ace Architects, on Second Street in Oakland, California, taxi drivers have no trouble homing in on the destination. "It's an architect's building," is the comment often made about the building, with its skewed glass façade, red-and-white-checkered metal-siding protrusion, silo-capped roof line, and exuberant fire stairs. At first, the location of the main door is a mystery; it lies ambiguously under the stairs. Once inside, however, the initial brutality of the exterior is offset by the excitement of the unusual interior spaces. Lucia Howard, 51 percent owner of the seven-person architectural firm, explains that the architectural imagery is literal. From her third-floor office, she points out the view of San Francisco Bay. "The Leviathan represents a sea monster which has crawled onto land. The creature's body is expressed in various architectural elements," she says, pointing to interior metal armatures that are its "ribs." She adds, "The point about our work is that we try to have fun, but we like to be pragmatic too."

Howard and her maverick partner, David Weingarten, who have been a team since they met at the University of California, Berkeley, where they both graduated with master of architecture degrees in 1978, make waves by vehemently opposing the abstraction of Modern architecture. Howard likes to take subjects from any area of life and transform them into architecture. Some of her most successful work has been in the retail field, where she learned to overcome spatial or site problems and create interiors that sell merchandise. The Country Store, a retailer of country-style housewares located on San Francisco's Pier 39, is a case in point. The boutique was positioned at the back of the retail development, making it difficult to attract passersby. Shoppers had to be drawn there by word of mouth and consumer enthusiasm. Howard's solution was to create a colorful juxtaposition of interior city- and countryscapes, divided by a distorted fairy-tale house of seven gables. It was a stage set for shopping in a fantasyland, and its success led to commissions for five other small stores, which together became the local equivalent of Disneyland. "The management was trying not just to make money but to make the whole pier work better," Howard remarks. In her design for the Lakeside Delicatessen, Howard's strategy was to juxtapose "good taste" and "bad taste"—a commentary on the "good food"–"bad food" dichotomy often found in the ethnic eateries of America. Logic and absurdity, cheap and expensive, were contained within a rotunda, creating an elegant yet exotic atmosphere.

From such small beginnings business flourished, and with it, commissions and awards flowed in. After fourteen years in business, the firm has now completed about fifty store interiors. In 1986 Howard was honored as one of the Forty Under Forty designers chosen by Philip Johnson and Robert A.M. Stern for outstanding work during the previous decade. In 1991 she was included in *Architectural Digest's* list of 100 architects while she was engaged in the mammoth task of reconfiguring four and a half miles of streetscape in San Jose, California, improving the façades of approximately seventy retail buildings for $10,000 each ("We can help retailers to get more mileage out of their small businesses."), as well as renovating Berkeley's old beaux-arts-style city hall.

While the playful nature of much of Howard's work is eminently suitable for publication and thereby attracts media attention, the underlying thought process is far from frivolous. Its intellectual underpinnings can be traced to her years of rigorous academic study at Wellesley College and the Massachusetts Institute of Technology, prior to attending UC Berkeley. Howard comments, "Our work is serious, although many of our critics say it isn't real architecture. We think the rest of the stuff isn't worth doing." She is intent on three crusades: to make architecture more accessible to people; to get serious recognition for women in the design professions; and to make a better world. "Architecture has been remote, and kept in a box so that only initiates could get it out and understand it," notes Howard. "My work is controversial because I have attempted to be adventurous. People ask how can I get away with it, but I believe that buildings should arouse positive emotions like laughter and joy. They should make people want to smile and dance, heighten awareness. We want to affirm life, speak to the optimism of the human [part] of the human spirit."

To help women gain recognition, Howard spends much of her time working with groups such as the San Francisco Organization of Women Architects and California Women in Environmental Design. Through seminars and exhibitions open to the general public, she helps to further understanding about women's contributions to the field. Howard explains that "house design, residential interiors, and the decorative arts are widely held to be the natural province of women designers. The belief that women are only interested in design as an extension of home economics permeates the minds of an enormous number of Americans. Just as statistics of two-wage-earner families finally laid to rest the idea that most women don't work, so the ongoing effort to exhibit and publish the work of women designers will demonstrate that they do not spend the majority of their time on houses." Howard notes that women seem to be carrying the baton in the nineties in the field of literature, with contemporary women writers, including a high percentage of minority women, taking the lead from Jewish men. Similarly, the tide is turning in architecture and design. "Though archi-

tecture and design move more slowly than other creative endeavors, we can already identify influential women, and the hum of this phenomenon is rising in all fields of design," Howard notes. The Bay Area, she points out, is well ahead of the rest of the country in the number and prominence of women-owned firms, many of which are well known.

In an effort "to make the world a better place," Howard devotes time to volunteer efforts, such as the recent campaign to preserve the Marin County Civic Center, a Frank Lloyd Wright–designed building that was in danger of being "violated" by a new building positioned in front of it. "We did a lot of beating the bushes, getting people out for demonstrations, and staved it off, supporting an alternative plan to put the new building underground," she explains. Studies of environmentally appropriate products have led her to use building materials that are cost-effective, nonpolluting, and support recycling. These include strand board, which looks like plywood but is made of waste-wood products; tile that looks like terrazzo chips but is made from waste-plastic material; low-voltage lighting; and low-"E" glass. Extra insulation is always applied and high-tech systems installed to control energy use.

While Howard acknowledges that only "secure" people will come to her firm, because she doesn't create "safe" solutions, she believes there is more support for what she does than other professionals imagine. Today, she insists, most people see architecture as a menace that takes away space and is an undesirable background for life. They have become dead to architecture and design. Pejorative expressions in everyday language—such as "shut the door on me" or "up against the wall"—are architectural metaphors pointing to a culture that has formed natural reactions against buildings. Howard insists that "there has to be another direction, toward restoring literalism in buildings, making them a framework for thinking about social and cultural institutions." If she has her way, the images will be of monsters, toys, forests, boats, and planes. And there is at least one sign suggesting that this will come to pass: Howard's business card is in the form of a playing card with an ace of spades. Clearly, she's out to trump the competition and the profession every time.

A selection of Howard's work appears on pages 198 to 203.

JOHN HALL

Naomi **Leff**

There are exotic orchids in the vase on the reception desk, wide wood planking with a soft, glowing patina stretches across the floor, and sunlight streams in through a skylight. Two of Frank Gehry's cardboard chair designs are lined up to receive visitors if they fancy sitting on collectors' pieces, and there is a soft leather couch for those who want to sink in and observe the passing scene. Well-dressed women are scurrying to and fro. The atmosphere is almost like that of a haute couture salon and has the same air of creativity, with the "couturiere" hidden behind the scenes, directing the staff to even higher levels of invention. When Naomi Leff, the president of this establishment, appears, exquisitely dressed in Armani grays and blues, with little jewelry to compete with her golden-red hair, the fashion analogy becomes even more pronounced.

Indeed, Leff's love of fashion has been a driving force since she went into business on her own in 1980 with three people, at a time when at least one of every two small businesses was failing within two years. Wisely, however, she decided to pursue an entrepreneurial rather than an artistic route, based upon her conviction that if women were truly "liberated," they should be able to go it alone and survive. With thirty-eight people on the payroll today, a 4,500-square-foot office in midtown Manhattan, and clients such as Ralph Lauren, Gucci, Anne Klein, Christian Dior, Saks Fifth Avenue, and Giorgio Armani, for whom she creates award-winning retail environments, she has proved that business intelligence is definitely part of the equation. Early on, she signed up for seminars run by the American Woman's Economic Development (AWED). She also received management and technical assistance from consultant Paul Sprague, president of Warwick Group Inc., which, she admits, was crucial to her success. Lacking any formal business education, and finding it difficult to be assertive, Leff focused on accumulating business skills—or as AWED puts it, filling in the blanks left by a feminine upbringing.

Leff never allowed herself to be thought of as a " 'woman decorator'—I looked on decorating as superficial and not highly professional, although I have since gained renewed respect for some extraordinary decorators in the field"—concentrating instead on issues of volume and space, producing very good architectural drawings, and displaying a truly professional capability in terms of an entire job. This professionalism has won her respect from a long roster of male CEO clients, who will often call on her for advice about the smallest detail of a multi-million-dollar project, confident that she will guide them correctly. And there is considerable satisfaction, too, knowing that she has gone further than the stereotypical woman architect who—at the time when she graduated from Pratt (1973) with a master's of science in environmental design, following undergraduate studies in architecture—was all too often relegated to doing bathroom fixtures.

Leff's path to her present pinnacle is an inspiring example of fortitude and determination. While she was a student at the Bronx School of Science, it was quickly determined that she had strong three-dimensional design talents, but a visiting pro-

Above: Holt Renfrew department store interiors, Toronto, Ontario. Photograph by John Hall.

Above: Gulfstream IV airplane interior. Photograph by John Hall.

fessor of architecture discouraged her from architecture "because it was a man's profession." Instead, she became a grade-school teacher who, in her off hours, promptly discarded cap and gown for paintbrush and canvas at the Arts Students League, or pencil and tracing paper at the New York School of Interior Design. She began doing small decorating jobs for friends and working *pro bono* for community centers in under-privileged neighborhoods. When one of her designs won an award, she knew it was time to give up teaching and start working toward her objective: to become a professional designer.

After completing a three-year postgraduate program at Pratt, Leff joined the office of John Carl Warnecke Associates, where she spent six years working on retail design (including stores for Neiman-Marcus and Bergdorf Goodman), which was eventually to become her niche market. When the dynamic CEO of Bloomingdale's, Marvin Traub, approached her to open a store-design division in 1975, she was not altogether convinced she should take his offer—it seemed to be selling out to commercialism—but women friends, including Susana Torre, now chairman of the environmental design department at Parsons School of Design, pointed out that it would be a learning experience. And it was. Leff recalls, "Salespeople would call me and say they hadn't earned a dollar in sales from one particular square foot of merchandising space, and I would be asked to correct the problem, through display design. It was wonderful to become a retailer and understand those issues."

Leff discovered that making SKUs (stock-keeping units) move off the floor was as important as the aesthetics of store design; she learned to marry business and visual appeal. Leff stayed at Bloomingdale's for five years, in a period when the store was exploiting the art of merchandising to its fullest. Bloomingdale's set the standards from which other retailers took their cues, introducing atmosphere, sensuality, and excitement into store environments that had previously been bland.

With a strong desire to be her own boss, as well as to diversify her design work, Leff opened her own firm with two projects on the boards—the offices for Cathy Cash Spellman, and a store for Simco shoes. "All my contacts said they were going to give me work, but they didn't say when," she recalls. A major breakthrough came, however, when J. P. Stevens launched a competition for a showroom design for Ralph Lauren's brand-new Home Collection in 1983. It was an opportunity to express everything Leff had learned about merchandising. She applied the principles and got the job.

The Leff touch employed the sensuous approach. A series of themed rooms were developed (to be changed periodically via interior design and different merchandise) for buyers to walk through: Thoroughbred, Attic, New England, Log Cabin, and Jamaica. They all spun the same Lauren story, of casual rusticity with an upscale "preppie" quality. They set out the "dreamscape" parameters to which all retailers selling Lauren home fashions had to adhere. All the fixtures, using honey pine paneling, moldings, and furniture, were designed by Leff, for eventual integration into stores. It was a total package that launched a mega-million-dollar business. Lauren's gratitude for this creative effort has been reflected in his ongoing relationship with Leff, who has designed nine stores for him, including those in France, Germany, Canada, and Japan.

In terms of prestige, none has been more impressive than the Madison Avenue store, housed in a landmark 1895 mansion. Here Lauren developed the jewel of his retail crown, a 20,000-square-foot environment that encourages customers to wander through four of the mansion's five floors. The fact that it looks so authentic is testament to Leff's capabilities. When she first walked through the aging, decrepit house, which had been disastrously carved up into thirty-two retail units, she recalls, there was only one ceiling in good shape, and it was impossible to believe that the mansion had once been a single-family house. Lauren wanted the mansion fully restored to its former glory, with the feel of a private home, and he wanted this done in just five months, which initially seemed totally impossible.

By thinking big—for example, producing ninety different crown moldings for the client to select from, ordering 82,000 feet of Honduras mahogany so that the interior would be consistent throughout, just like a townhouse, and re-creating what seems to be the original staircase out of a space that was occupied by an air-conditioning unit—Leff created (on schedule!) an interior that even had her client change out of his normal well-worn jeans into a double-breasted gray suit, striped shirt, and silk tie for opening day. It also won her the chance to work with Lauren on two of his private residences.

During the past five years, retail projects have been augmented with further residential work, corporate jets, hotels, and conference centers. A temporary clubhouse in Windsor, the Florida enclave created by Prince Charles with his polo-playing international friends, is a project Leff is particularly pleased with: "It's Victorian, romantic, and glamorous. It has a comfortable English colonial look, with fans, rattan, crystal, and glass. It's not full of presumptuous furniture." A sense of place, of Florida, evident in this project, has led to commissions for several other houses in this exclusive development.

A love of fashion, Leff believes, makes her appreciate changes of style, so that she never wants to be typecast in terms of design or ideas. Just because something worked in the past does not mean it will work again in the future. In fact, she feels that as "an entrepreneur who designs," it is almost her responsibility to conceptualize new trends and bring them to the marketplace. Squarely on her mind these days are new directions in retailing. She believes that "horizontal" shopping (i.e., on one level) will be favored over "vertical shopping" in the 1990s. "If I'm asked for advice," she remarks, "I will tell my department-store clients to sell off their top floors and buy the block. People want to get in and out of a destination fast, but they still want to shop in one location. I'd love to help someone do this." She adds with her acquired businesslike assertiveness, "I just know I'm right."

A selection of Leff's work appears on pages 204 to 209.

TOD GILFORD

Phyllis
Martin-Vegue

Above: Green Library, Stanford University, Stanford, California. Photograph by Jane Lidz.

The new Main Library of San Francisco will be completed in 1995, and the story of how the architects won the commission for this multi-million-dollar building is a testament to the professionalism of Phyllis Martin-Vegue and her partners, Cathy Simon, Lamberto Moris, and Peter Winkelstein. Long before the official RFPs (requests for proposals) went out, the partners investigated what the city officials were looking for. It turned out that they wanted a world-class architect who would joint-venture with a local San Francisco design firm. "We decided *we* wanted to be the local design firm," recalls Martin-Vegue, "so we then set about identifying a major architecture firm we thought would be prominent enough to get the job and who we would like to work with. We finally settled on I. M. Pei's firm, Pei Cobb Freed & Partners." Simon Martin-Vegue Winkelstein Moris then contacted the Pei office and suggested the joint venture. "They were not aware of the project and were delighted to know about it," explains Martin-Vegue. "They agreed to the joint-venture arrangement."

And the rest, as they say, is history. Despite stiff competition, the firm's proposal won the commission, a coup for Martin-Vegue and her partners, considering that they have only been in business since 1985. "This is the way we like to work, getting involved early on with brainstorming about interiors," she remarks. "We often get hired when a building is under construction, which is a disadvantage and can be costly to a client. We don't want to deal with what's left over after the building has been finished."

The lesson here is that subtle, businesslike marketing pays off, and Martin-Vegue believes that insistence on such strategies in no way compromises the status of a design firm but often can be enhancing, producing a more integrated result. "Design is everything, the thing we all live for, but you have to earn a living and have a viable business while you practice," she says determinedly. It was, indeed, this policy that resulted in the formation of the firm. All four partners were working in another office in San Francisco before they split off, taking twenty-seven people with them. "We had asked to put the firm on a sound financial footing, we wanted more control over our lives, but the principals wouldn't listen to us," Martin-Vegue explains. "We negotiated for six months, and then we left. It was a tough decision to make after working at one place for fifteen years, like a divorce, very painful, and it still is tough, because we now compete against our old firm, and our former boss is very bitter about that."

One of the first items on the fledgling firm's agenda was financial planning. "We knew we were all creative people with less than a clue about how to handle money, so we found an adviser who set up our entire business plan. It has worked ever since. And our firm no longer lives from moment to moment, without jobs on the horizon, wondering what's in the future." Simon and Winkelstein head up the architectural side of this full-service firm, and Martin-Vegue and Moris handle the interiors, with Dianne Filippi serving as chief administrative officer. "We're five very different people and probably would not have chosen each other, but our talents are complementary so it is very successful," Martin-Vegue explains. "This is not a star-oriented firm. Every Wednesday at noon we have a forum to critique and an opportunity for anyone in the project to get involved."

Despite her growing up with an architect father, Martin-Vegue never wanted to be an architect herself. From age thirteen, when her father allowed her to decorate her own room in the new house he designed for the family, she always preferred interior design. Early on, however, she decided not to get involved in residential work but to concentrate on commercial design: "I did not want to be the "go-between" between a husband and wife. A house should be a personal statement. I'm not interested in psychodrama; I am more interested in philosophical statements about public life."

She left her home state of Michigan after graduating in 1964 with a bachelor of science degree in design from the University of Michigan College of Architecture and Design, determined to see San Francisco and then tour Europe. "I found San Francisco so seductive that I never left," she laughs. "It is a liberal city, and there has always been more opportunity for minorities. As a woman principal in business, I find that women are now coming into power in this city. They have evolved into higher levels of business compared to other cities in the country. This makes a difference for me now, as many of my clients are women. This is wonderful because we talk the same language, network together, and help each other. It has never been like that before."

When Martin-Vegue first worked in the city in 1964, there were, she recalls, two formulas for interior design: overdecorated (frou-frou and flowery chintz) or underdecorated (ultramodern). She thought she could do a better job, "because little attention was paid to color. Some people believe that fashion influences color in design, but I don't think that innovative design is influenced by trends. You work out your own ideas, and go and get it done somehow, even if it doesn't exist in the marketplace."

Martin-Vegue heads up a department of fifteen people (doubled since the firm was established) within a forty-person firm. Her group concentrates equally on three areas of design: corporate offices; institutional projects, such as hospitals, libraries, and campus buildings; and hospitality projects. Twenty-five percent of this work comes from in-house architectural projects, the remainder from outside. Twenty to thirty projects are on the boards simultaneously. There is no signature design strategy, and no "look," because Martin-Vegue believes that a project should be responsive to the individual needs of

Above: Cheeca Lodge, Islamorada, Florida. Photograph by Mark Darley/Esto.

the client and the site: "One of our philosophical attitudes is to be contextual. We don't create out of thin air. We collect colors from the site—brick, stones, plant material, earth, whatever is there. Then we look at the surrounding architecture, the detailing of roof gutters, the materials, and from all this information we begin to build a color palette. It is an intellectual thought process, just as it is in architecture."

A certain aspect predominates in any Martin-Vegue project, however, and this is the floor, which is often her creative starting point. Each project will include at least one custom-designed rug or carpet, or an intricate marble-inlaid patterned floor surface, which may complement the softer surfaces. The level of creativity will vary from one project to the next, but each will be unique. For a hotel such as Le Meridien in Chicago, where a lobby piano bar was designed as a central gathering point, Martin-Vegue introduced a black-and-white piano-key motif, which was reiterated in the floor of the foyer, done in a complex assembly of marbles, as well as the foyer rug, the custom wall-to-wall carpeting in the piano lobby itself, and the conferencing facilities on another level in the hotel. It was a sophisticated visual theme for a sophisticated boutique hotel, which featured all-white bathrooms, with European hardware for the sinks and tubs. (The hotel, by the way, has won numerous awards.)

For a corporate office job, the floor will often be carpeted and bordered in several colors—her own office offers a gray carpet with intense purple borders and a red dash design. In a more sedate institutional situation, such as the Olin School of the Humanities at Bard College, small cut-out squares of color are inserted in a random pattern in the wall-to-wall gray carpet. At Stanford University's Green Library, muted terracotta is bordered with vanilla, with a narrow purple stripe in between. Martin-Vegue can seemingly come up with endless ideas and interpretations for the flooring, which she considers "one of the biggest opportunities to express color." She points out, "Walls are so often covered with neutral fabric or texture. Ceilings are not a design opportunity except for lighting. The floor is the one plane that is available to make a statement and do something wonderful."

A selection of Martin-Vegue's work appears on pages 210 to 213.

Margaret **McCurry**

Above: Stairway, Chicago Bar Association. Photograph by Bruce Van Inwegen.

I t is early on a Monday morning and the phone is ringing in the offices of Tigerman McCurry, located in a loft building in Chicago. The secretary refers the caller, an important developer client, Paul Beitler, to Margaret McCurry, who hears that he wants immediate schematics for the design of a new building for the Chicago Bar Association. Can they be on his desk by Friday? McCurry welcomes the challenge. Her partner, Stanley Tigerman, is away in Japan and will not be back by Friday. It will be her responsibility to get the job done—and it is the firm's first opportunity to build a high-rise anywhere. Beitler is suggesting about thirty floors on a tight site down-town, adjacent to the new Chicago Public Library. He is also clear about what he wants: something a little Gothic to please the American Bar Association, which is hardly what Tigerman McCurry is used to producing. The firm is known for strong statements in the Miesian Modern and Postmodern idioms. Still, this is not the moment to argue a point of philosophy. There are not that many opportunities to build big.

Taking a disciplined approach to the task, and leaning heavily on her past experience at the Chicago office of Skidmore Owings & Merrill, where she worked closely with master architect Bruce Graham learning how to plan out a big building in repetitive bays, McCurry does the schematics, presents the proposal—and gets the job.

The idea of "getting on with it" has been the leitmotif throughout McCurry's career, ever since she left Vassar College in 1964 with a bachelor's degree in art history and set out to seek her fortune at twenty-one. Although her father was in practice in Chicago as a partner in the architectural firm of Schmidt, Gardner & Erickson, she did not consciously decide to follow in his footsteps. Her early experience was in packaging design, but it was when she began to see boxes displayed on shelves that she started to think about buildings and interiors.

She joined SOM in 1966 and spent the next eleven years there, absorbing the wisdom of partners Graham and Walter Netsch and working with associate partner Davis Allen on interiors. All around her were designers who were to become legends in later decades: George Larson, Diane Legge Kemp (the first woman to become a full partner at SOM in 1982), Patrick McConnell, Donald Powell, Robert Kleinschmidt, and Natalie du Blois. "I was the only one who did not have a title, because, as they kept pointing out, I was not educated," she recalls. "Dave Allen taught me how to handle my frustrations. He used to tell me to relax and enjoy life, and when he didn't need me, he'd tell me to go out to a museum. Looking back, it was a happy time. I was paid to learn."

Among the major projects she worked on were the Container Corporation headquarters (1968), the National Life & Accident Insurance Company headquarters (1968–77), the St. Joseph Valley Bank (1972–74), the Baxter Laboratories headquarters (1974–76) and the Holiday Inn Mart Plaza in Chicago (1975–77). They were all rigorous, large-scale buildings that required her to relate to the larger architectural picture and contribute ideas on furniture, finishing materials, such as tile and hardware, and indoor plants. She became fully accustomed to sitting in meetings with mechanical engineers, lighting consultants, structural engineers, and other technical experts and had the chance to learn how a building was put together both on and off the job site. There was client-contact work as well—"I learned how to handle boards of directors by letting them have consensus"—in addition to the business and budget aspects of a job—"all part of making sure the project worked out properly."

In the 1977 economic downturn, when she was let go and forced to open her own one-person office out of her studio apartment, she found she fit smoothly into the gap "between decorators and architects" in the residential market. "People were needing more done than decorators could do." Adding to her qualifications, she took the National Council of Interior Design Qualification (NCIDQ) exam, and then, in 1979, with proof of a legitimate apprenticeship in architecture behind her, she studied for her architectural registration exam, and passed.

By then she had met (and married) Stanley Tigerman, who was beginning to have an effect on her architecture, just as Allen had influenced her interpretations of interior design. While Allen introduced her to a "looser vocabulary, away from the die-hard Miesians" and taught her that antiques were important, as were ideas from periods other than Modern, Tigerman gave her insights into his personal design philosophy, the interplay of the sacred and the profane, which he called "opposites of the same mirror."

She joined his firm as a partner in 1982 (after winning her first major award from *Interiors* for a job done independently for Chicago's Van Straaten Art Gallery), and together she and Tigerman expressed a radically irreverent ideology in a series of projects. These included a prototypical office plan executed for *Interiors* magazine, which introduced the concept of "outdoors indoors," down to cardboard cutout clouds over the workstations and artificial turf on the floor; a pseudo-Palladian scheme for their own offices, with a yellow-domed ceiling and all the staff in white surgical coats; and their own award-winning lakeside house, constructed in brutal corrugated metal but set in an idyllic landscape, with a wicket gate and a serpentine wooden walkway to the front door. These were brave iconoclastic statements, and they helped to move the practice

 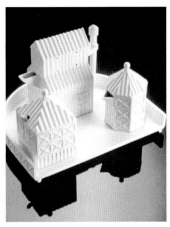

Above: Heritage Line of faucets designed by McCurry and Stanley Tigerman for American Standard.

Above: Tigerman McCurry's "Teaside" coffee and tea service, manufactured by Swid Powell. Photograph by Tom Wedell.

firmly onto center stage, resulting in prestigious invitations to design objects such as tableware and silverware for Alessi and Swid Powell, with the opportunity for royalty sales and publicity that brought them public prominence, and a colossal commission for an American Standard showroom, budgeted at $1.2 million, which they designed with full working plumbing and cascades of continuously falling water.

Personally, however, McCurry describes her own work as organized and controlled but "with a mood or feeling touching on the traditional that people seem to fall in love with. Stanley has shown me how to bring all levels of meaning and history to whatever I do. I've learned that eclectic is okay." She likes clients who are looking for "gentler things and enjoy American vernacular furniture and cottages." This is not to say that she cannot bring a very sophisticated urban touch to a project when necessary. Her design of the Herman Miller office furniture showroom, unveiled at the 1984 Neocon exhibition at the Chicago Merchandise Mart, was a stunning assemblage of materials—brick, mosaic tile, timber, and leather—that won a local Chicago chapter AIA award. And the ground-floor lobby of the Chicago Bar Association building is a distillation of Chicago 1930s' moderne, with all the iconography that lawyers can relate to—floors of geometrically patterned marble, detailing in stainless steel, capacious armchairs upholstered in aqua-blue velvet, and sandblasted glass light fixtures.

Aware of her responsibilities to the profession, particularly since she was inducted into *Interior Design* magazine's Hall of Fame in 1990, McCurry devotes a good deal of time to lecturing at various institutions and contributes long-range planning to the National AIA Committee on Design, for which she will be the first woman chairperson in 1993. As she herself points out, "Women have come a long way from beehive hairdos and gloves and hats over the last thirty years."

A selection of McCurry's work appears on pages 214 to 217.

Above: No detail was overlooked in creating the flagship Regent Hotel in Milan, Italy, which involved the renovation of a fourteenth-century monastery. A luxurious marble bathroom is generously mirrored to expand the space. The glass lighting fixtures were custom made in Venice. Photograph by Aldo Ballo.

Left: For the offices of a San Francisco law firm, the orchestration of interior components creates a quiet sense of luxury. Sandblasted glass block, classic Barcelona chairs, blonde sycamore wood, an expansive terrazzo floor, and an antique Persian rug, along with selected works of art, were carefully chosen to keep the mood light, yet rich. Photograph by Toshi Yoshimi.

Opposite: The Netherlands headquarters of Shell, in The Hague, is often called one of the finest corporate interior spaces completed during the 1980s. Babey and her partner, the late Charles Pfister, worked on 50,000 square feet on four floors: one for dining and entertaining; two for offices; and the top floor for meetings. An effort was made to accommodate the Dutch love of light and intimate spaces, and to add touches of the country's traditional heritage to the modern structure, designed by the Skidmore Owings & Merrill firm. In one of the small dining rooms, a Delft theme was embraced, with a display of plates and tiles on one wall. The lighting fixture was custom made in Venice. Fortuny silk wall panels are separated by half-round beads of white gold leaf. Antique Dutch chairs are upholstered in leather. Photograph by Jaime Ardiles-Arce.

Above: Mohair-upholstered seating, a red lacquer conference table, and an wall-hung Edo-period Japanese screen are the highlights of this informal lounge and conference area in the Shell headquarters. Photograph by Jaime Ardiles-Arce.

Right: This informal space, designed for use by Shell employees as a place to hold receptions or other company get-togethers, has a deliberately residential feeling. By installing oversize "peacock" chairs, a less corporate atmosphere is created, a contrast to the functional look applied to "working" spaces. Photograph by Jaime Ardiles-Arce.

Opposite: An intricately patterned Fortuny cotton fabric covers the walls in a director's office at the Shell project. Thai silk covers the sofa and pillows; granite tops the table. The selected textures and colors create a certain, and rather unexpected, coziness in the space. Photograph by Jaime Ardiles-Arce.

Above: Latticework in the circular
lounge area of the Doubletree Hotel
Plaza Las Fuentes, in Pasadena,
California, creates the feeling of a
gazebo. The outdoor atmosphere is
further emphasized by the use of
wicker furnishings. Photograph by
Jaime Ardiles-Arce.

Opposite: The ambience of an old-
fashioned grand hotel in the tropics
is presented in this double-height
hallway at the Doubletree. The
immense chandeliers were designed
by Babey and handmade in Venice
especially for the project. Photograph by Jaime Ardiles-Arce.

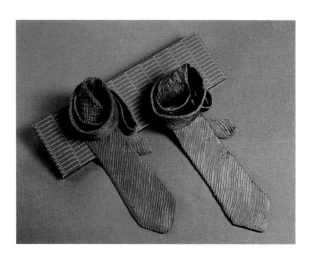

Top left: Camp, a wool fabric from Bellinger's Adirondack Collection, is a classic buffalo plaid produced in several colors. Photograph by Bill Kontzias.

Top right: Camp covers the chairs and was used to create the suit worn by its designer in an advertisement. Photograph by John Stembler.

Center left: Bellinger's elegantly tactile Isadora, a pleated 100 percent silk fabric, is offered in thirteen rich colors. Photograph by Bill Kontzias.

Center right: The company made these neckties out of Isadora pleated silk fabric as a promotional gift. Photograph by Bill Kontzias.

Bottom left: Bellinger's classic Limousine Cloth is a staple of corporate specifiers around the world and is offered in several tones. Photograph by Paul Pearl.

Bottom right: Fabrics from the Bellinger collection, including Isadora pleated silk, used for draperies, and Limousine Cloth, which covers the sofa, were used in creating a stylish Manhattan living room for the designer. Bellinger worked closely with architects Powell/Kleinschmidt on the project. Photograph by Peter Aaron/Esto.

*Above: A clean-lined sense of purity
pervades the textiles designed by
Bellinger, and that signature look
also characterizes the spaces in
which the designer lives and works,
as the design studio section of the
Gretchen Bellinger Inc offices indicates. The firm is housed in a renovated nineteenth-century warehouse
building in Cohoes, New York.
Photograph by Peter Aaron/Esto.*

Above: Bellinger's taste for clear, clean forms and understated elegance is apparent in the design of her New York City residence. Textiles of her own design on display include Arcadia plain weave on the walls, Limousine Cloth broadcloth on the sofa, Josephine iridescent silk on chairs, and Scheherazade silk herringbone and Pullman Cloth èpingle on pillows. Photograph by Peter Aaron/Esto.

Above: The subtle combination of textures and colors creates a stunningly handsome bedroom in the designer's Manhattan apartment. Among the Bellinger fabrics used are Pasha linen velvet for the bedcover, Gibraltar textured weave on the headboard, Scheherazade silk herringbone bolsters and upholstered wall, and Corde du Roi vertical cut-pile pillows. Photograph by Peter Aaron/Esto.

Opposite: The "Fish and Flora"
bedroom at Camp Bellinger, outfitted with a headboard upholstered in
Arcadia plain weave, bolsters in
Garlands, a silk jacquard fabric,
pillows in Isadora pleated silk,
and a Yachting Cotton coverlet.
Photograph by Peter Aaron/Esto.

Above: The great room at Camp
Bellinger, the designer's lakeside
estate in the Adirondacks, has been
newly redecorated by Bellinger,
employing an array of her fabrics,
including Camel woven herringbone for windowseat cushions,
Thistledorn textured weave for
bolsters, and Durant deerskin and
Hiawatha hereford slunk for pillows.
Sofa cushions and bolsters are
Guideboat cotton bouclé; pillows
are covered in Porch canvas stripe.
Wicker chair cushions are covered
in Cotswold plain weave. Photograph by Peter Aaron/Esto.

Top: A colorful "birdhouse" mail-
box adds a bit of interest to an
office corridor at Viacom. Photograph by Elliot Kaufman.

Above: In the New York City offices
of Viacom, a project planned by
Conway and designed by her former
KPFC partner J. Woodson Rainey,
Jr., the playful and lighthearted
spirit of the entertainment organization is captured. The elevator
lobby space of the MTV division
is capped by a distinctive pitched-
roof structure. Photograph by Elliot
Kaufman.

Left: The reception area for the
Nickelodeon cable channel, whose
programming caters to younger
viewers, has an appropriately
whimsical feeling. Photograph
by Elliot Kaufman.

Right: The central reception area of the Cleary, Gottlieb, Steen & Hamilton law offices is handsomely detailed. Conway spent two years programming and planning this New York City project prior to its design by her former firm, KPFC. Photograph by Paul Warchol.

Below right: Specially crafted pieces of furniture are grouped together in an executive reception area at MONY Financial Services Headquarters, New York City. Conway's former partner Richard Kronick turned to craftspeople for input on this major corporate project, in an effort to bring warmth and personality to the business environment. Photograph by Paul Warchol.

Opposite: A contemporary sense of glamour welcomes visitors in the reception space of the offices of a private investment partnership in New York City. The 12,000-squarefoot space was designed by Conway's former partner J. Woodson Rainey, Jr. Photograph by Peter Aaron/Esto.

Left: The lobby of MONY Financial Services Headquarters in midtown Manhattan is a grand, double-height space executed in substantial materials—marble, steel, and mahogany—to reinforce the firm's image of substance and security. Conway and Miguel Valcarcel were the KPFC partners in charge. Conway's former partner Paul Rosen was the designer. Photograph by Paul Warchol.

Below left: A custom-designed bench along one wall of the MONY lobby reiterates the space's theme of strength and solidity. Photograph by Paul Warchol.

Opposite: A VIP lounge in Bally's Park Place Casino Hotel, Atlantic City, New Jersey, was developed in the vocabulary of a traditional grand hotel interior: vaulted ceiling, bronze-detailed marble columns, updated classic club chairs, and pendant lights. Conway's former partner Dan Stewart was project manager. Photograph by Paul Warchol.

Above: A reception area in the New York offices of Marsh & McLennan demonstrates the originality with which Halsband and her partner, Robert Kliment, approach lighting. A pendant luminaire over the reception desk contains both up- and downlighting. Photograph by Norman McGrath.

Left: A double-height hallway in the offices of Levine Huntley Schmidt & Beaver in Manhattan manipulates natural light effectively into the interior space. Photograph by Norman McGrath.

Opposite: In a modestly budgeted restaurant-design project in Woodstock, New York, walls were stenciled with leaf patterns colored to represent the seasons. The client received a handsome dining environment with a minimal investment in paint and labor. Photograph by Jon Naar.

Overleaf: The design of the studio space of a weekend house in Woodstock, New York, references the Arts and Crafts tradition of the Hudson Valley region. A William Morris–designed fabric covers the peaked ceiling, botanical prints enliven the walls, and wicker and wood furnishings add charm to the airy, light-filled space. Photograph by Langdon Clay.

Above: Ace Architects' "Psycho-Remodel" of a private residence in Berkeley, California, focused on the creation of a progression of rooms in which a variety of aesthetic experiences are produced. In the master bath, a dark and secluded atmosphere was realized. Against the background of marbleized walls, the arrangement of the tile on the walls offers a decorative look of studied randomness. The interior of a niche above the bathtub is painted with a classical-style scene. Photograph by Christopher Irion.

Opposite: The "Psycho-Remodel" bedroom is a glowing space, with a colorful trompe l'oeil painting of architecture and sky on the ceiling that changes one's perception of the room's geometric configuration. Photograph by David Livingston.

Above: In a private residence built on a steep site in the Montclair district of the Oakland hills, Howard's signature steel columns are used to create architectural substance along a patio wall. A stairway leads to a family room in the house, which expands upon the Spanish colonial revival character of its context. Photograph by Terry McCarthy.

Left: The study in a San Francisco residence is accessed from an ellipse-shaped foyer. The décor is the designer's attempt to reconstruct the so-called Bay Region style. Photograph by Christopher Irion.

Above: This pavilionlike space, which opens onto a multicolored slate patio, was added to an existing Berkeley, California, residence. Its character is created through the use of traditional Japanese construction methods, hardware from Asian markets, and other Far Eastern artifacts. Photograph by Richard Barnes.

Right: The interior elements of the Community Travel Service in Oakland, California, allude to varied travel instruments and experiences. The circular counter is suggestive of a compass; the seating in the waiting area is reminiscent of an ocean liner smokestack; the service desk, at right, is constructed to look like an old-fashioned railroad-station ticket counter. Photograph by Alan Weintraub.

Overleaf: The design of the garden at the Lakeside Delicatessen in Oakland, California, references classical architecture forms in contemporary materials. Steel columns form a pergola in this updated Elysianlike landscape. Photograph by Russell Abraham.

Left: The handsome sales areas of the Polo/Ralph Lauren shop on Rodeo Drive are arranged in a residential format, with details, such as a ceiling fan, that create a slightly more casual Southern California flavor. Though all-new construction, the Beverly Hills shop offers moldings and fine-quality woodwork that make the interiors appear as if they have been there for decades. Photograph by François Halard.

Top: In the Polo/Ralph Lauren flagship store, housed in the meticulously converted and restored Rhinelander mansion on Madison Avenue in New York City, Leff perfected the image vocabulary that the fashion and home-furnishings company has employed throughout the world in retail branches from Paris to Tokyo. Photograph by David Phelps.

Above: The charming courtyard of the Polo/Ralph Lauren retail store in Beverly Hills, California, demonstrates Leff's concern about creating the correct ambience for the classic clothing and accessories that the company sells. Photograph by François Halard.

Opposite: Colorado's Beaver Creek Conference Center complex is comprised of a three-story clubhouse surrounded by clusters of cottages. The facility is used for informal conferences for up to 150 people. A warm, residential atmosphere, executed in the vocabulary of the classic mountain lodge of the American West, was created. Rustic elements, such as the exposed timber walls, hunting trophies, Native American crafts, Western-theme works of art, and local river rock, used for the fireplace and chimney, successfully convey a sense of comfort and relaxation. Photograph by John Hall.

Above: At Beaver Creek, the pine-floored dining room, with its soaring forty-foot-high ceiling and mezzanine gallery hung with Indian rugs, is furnished to create a casual environment, encouraging informal conversation among guests. Photograph by John Hall.

Above and opposite: A shopping complex at the base of a major mixed-use building in New York City, The Arcade at Citicorp consists of a series of small shops. Crisp white tile floors are used throughout the project to create a sense of uniformity, while lighting effects and subtle graphics create a bright and welcoming environment in which to browse. Photograph by Jaime Ardiles-Arce.

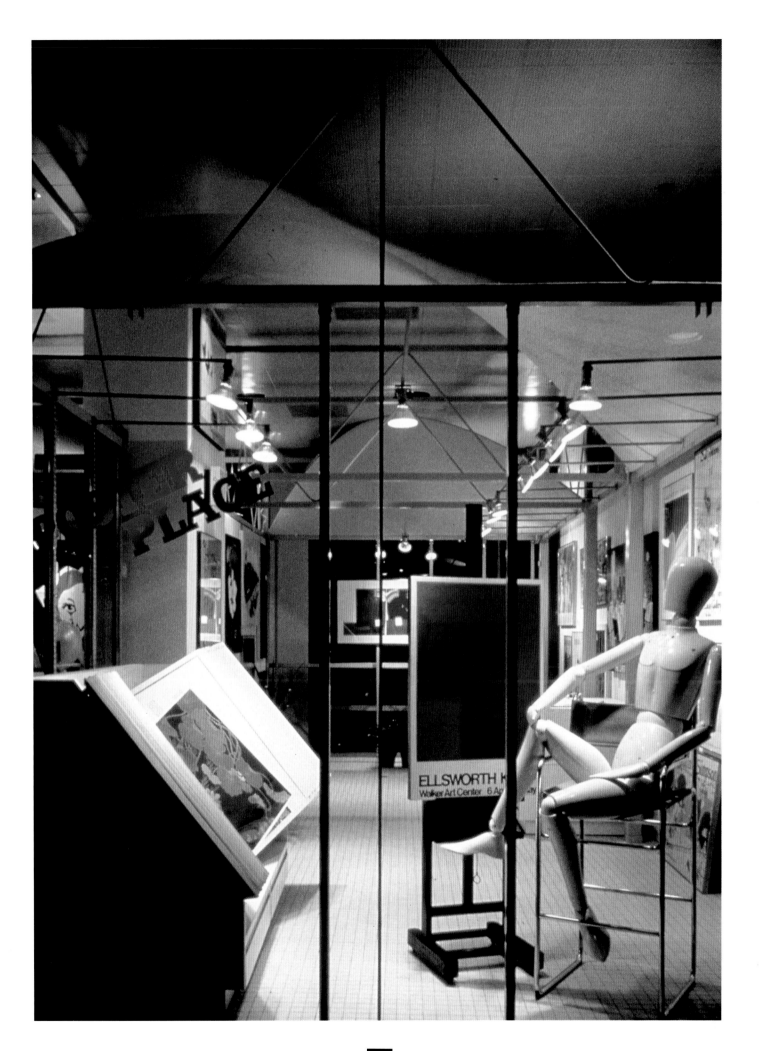

Above: Having established a strong corporate culture, Apple Computer demanded the articulation of the company philosophy in the design of its facility in Campbell, California. A fanciful graphic composition in the reception area involves the reflection of the ceiling's geometry in the four-color carpet custom designed by Martin-Vegue. Photograph by Chas McGrath.

Right: The playful colorations at Apple Computer continue in circulation spaces, with custom-designed carpeting by Martin-Vegue delineating interior spaces. Photograph by Chas McGrath.

Opposite: Reflected in a four-story-high mirrored wall, the atrium lobby floor at the Hotel Le Meridien in Chicago is covered with a carpet designed by Martin-Vegue that organizes the space. Its diamond and "piano-key" motifs echo those seen in traditional Chicago-style interiors. Photograph by Mark Darley.

Opposite: The Highlands Inn in
Carmel-by-the-Sea, California,
has undergone several renovations
during its sixty-year history. For
its most recent renovation program,
Martin-Vegue's interior design team
was consulted early on by architect
Will Shaw, principal of Shaw
Associates, the firm in charge of
the entire project. A soft palette
of beige, misty green, and grayed
lavender was selected, alluding to
the colors of the rock, sea, sunsets,
and the forestlike environment
which surrounds the hotel and
conference center. Photograph by
Russell Abraham.

Above: The Cheeca Lodge in
Islamorada, Florida, is a prestigious island fishing retreat. Its
recent renovation called for retain-
ing its "clubby" quality while em-
phasizing the region's character.
Materials, such as native Florida
Key–stone flooring, and a seaside
color scheme assist in the creation
of the desired effect. Photograph
by Mark Darley/Esto.

Above: For a weekend house built on Lake Michigan, McCurry was called upon to fulfill the complete architecture and interior design program. The result is a charming vernacular cottage, christened Wit's End. The rooms of the house are organized around a central sitting room, intended to be "piazza-like" according to the designer. Bookshelves that flank the fireplace and generously scaled English-style chairs and sofa impart a sense of coziness to the space. Photograph by Bruce Van Inwegen.

Opposite: Dormers at Wit's End, in Sawyer, Michigan, assist in creating the cottage-style feeling desired by the owners. In an upstairs bathroom, the dormer provides a place for an architecturally interesting tub and shower area enclosed by glass partitions. The walls and peaked ceiling are fully tiled, creating a room within the room. Photograph by Bruce Van Inwegen.

Opposite: In a dramatic New York City showroom for the bath-fixture manufacturer American Standard, conceived as a series of black-and-white-tiled rooms, the product is graphically displayed on the walls, as well as in fully plumbed areas. A rigorous grid pattern is imposed on floors, walls, and ceilings. Photograph by Timothy Hursley.

Above: McCurry worked with partner Stanley Tigerman on the design for the Chicago Bar Association's sixteen-story headquarters—a case of almost instant gratification. The designers were given seven days to produce a design for a traditional-style building, in keeping with the history of the legal profession. The result is appropriately stately—inside and out. In this view, a circular entrance lobby capped by a silver-leafed ceiling leads into a clublike waiting area, offering rich wood detailing, a steel mantelpiece, and mohair-covered tub chairs. Photograph by Hedrich-Blessing.

Right: In the elevator lobby of the Chicago Bar Association, bronze elevator doors, etched with the insignia of the twelve tribes of Israel, are set off by veneered marble walls. Photograph by Bruce Van Inwegen.

Leslie Armstrong
Armstrong Cumming
118 West 22nd Street
New York, NY 10011
(212) 929-0164

Pamela Babey
Babey-Moulton
633 Battery Street
San Francisco, CA 94111
(415) 394-9910

Gretchen Bellinger
Gretchen Bellinger Inc
P.O. Box 64
Cohoes, NY 12047-0064
(518) 235-2828

Martha Burns
Fox & Fowle Architects
22 West 19th Street
New York, NY 10011
(212) 627-1700

Josephine Carmen/Clara Igonda
Carmen Farnum Igonda Design
1655 North Cherokee Avenue
Los Angeles, CA 90028
(213) 462-0993

Clodagh
Clodagh Design International
365 First Avenue
New York, NY 10010
(212) 673-9202

Patricia Conway
University of Pennsylvania Graduate School of Fine Arts
210 South 34th Street
Philadelphia, PA 19104-6311
(215) 898-8321

Karen Daroff
Daroff Design Inc.
2300 Ionic Street
Philadelphia, PA 19103
(215) 636-9900

Lee Foster-Crowder
Lee Foster-Crowder Design
1333 H Street NW
Washington, D.C. 20005
(202) 371-5529

Margo Grant
Gensler & Associates/Architects
1 Rockefeller Plaza
New York, NY 10020
(212) 581-9600

Carol Groh
149 Fifth Avenue
New York, NY 10011
(212) 529-8039

Frances Halsband
R. M. Kliment & Frances Halsband Architects
255 West 26th Street
New York, NY 10001
(212) 243-7400

Dorothy Harris
Dorothy Harris Interior Design
105 Hidden Valley Road
Fayetteville, GA 30214
(404) 461-2805

Kitty Hawks
Kitty Hawks, Inc.
136 East 57th Street
New York, NY 10022
(212) 832-3810

Margaret Helfand
Margaret Helfand Architects
32 East 38th Street
New York, NY 10016
(212) 779-7260

Lucia Howard
Ace Architects
The Leviathan
330 2nd Street
Oakland, CA 94607
(510) 452-0775

Carolyn Iu
Skidmore Owings & Merrill
333 Bush Street
San Francisco, CA 94104
(415) 981-1555

Naomi Leff
Naomi Leff & Associates
12 West 27th Street
New York, NY 10001
(212) 686-6300

Debra Lehman-Smith
Lehman-Smith Wiseman
1150 18th Street NW
Washington, DC 20036
(202) 466-5660

Dian Love
Payette Associates, Inc.
285 Summer Street
Boston, MA 02210
(617) 342-8200

Eva Maddox
Eva Maddox Associates
440 North Wells Street
Chicago, IL 60610
(312) 670-0092

Stephanie Mallis
Stephanie Mallis, Inc.
405 Lexington Avenue
New York, NY 10174
(212) 682-8045

Phyllis Martin-Vegue
Simon Martin-Vegue Winkelstein Moris
501 Second Street
San Francisco, CA 94107
(415) 546-0400

Elizabeth McClintock
MGS Architects
611 Broadway
New York, NY 10012
(212) 473-5334

Margaret McCurry
Tigerman McCurry
444 North Wells Street
Chicago, IL 60610
(312) 644-5880

Spes Mekus
Mekus-Johnson, Inc.
455 East Illinois Street
Chicago, IL 60611
(312) 661-0778

Julia Monk
Brennan Beer Gorman & Monk
515 Madison Avenue
New York, NY 10022
(212) 888-7667

Sylvia Owen
Owen & Mandolfo, Inc.
192 Lexington Avenue
New York, NY 10016
(212) 686-4576

Rita St. Clair
Rita St. Clair Associates
1009 North Charles Street
Baltimore, MD 21201
(301) 752-1313

Lella Vignelli
Vignelli Designs
475 Tenth Avenue
New York, NY 10018
(212) 244-1919

Lynn Wilson
Lynn Wilson Associates International
111 Majorca Avenue
Coral Gables, FL 33134
(305) 442-4041

Trisha Wilson
Wilson & Associates
3811 Turtle Creek Boulevard
Dallas, TX 75219-4419
(214) 521-6753

Anscome, Isabelle. *A Woman's Touch*. London: Virago Press, 1984.

Attfield, Judy and Part Kirkham. *A View from the Interior: Feminism, Women & Design*. London: Women's Press, 1989.

Barker Woolger, Jennifer and Roger J. Woolger. *The Goddess Within: A Guide to Eternal Myths that Shape Women's Lives*. New York: Fawcett Columbine, 1987.

Berkeley, Ellen Perry, editor, Matilda McQuaid, associate editor. *Architecture: A Place for Women*. Washington and London: Smithsonian Institution Press, 1989.

Blanke, Gail and Kathleen Walas. *Taking Control of Your Life: The Secrets of Successful Enterprising Women*. New York: MasterMedia, Avon Products, Inc., 1990.

Boutelle, Sara Holmes. *Julia Morgan Architect*. New York: Abbeville Press, 1988.

De Pree, D. J. *A Modern Consciousness: Florence Knoll*. Washington, D.C.: Smithsonian Institution Press, 1975.

De Wolfe, Elsie. *After All*. London and Toronto: William Heinemann, 1935.

Eisler, Riane. *The Chalice & The Blade: Our History, Our Future*. San Francisco: Harper & Row, 1987.

Gordon, Suzanne. *Prisoners of Men's Dreams: Striking out for a New Feminine Future*. Boston: Little, Brown, 1991.

Grattam, Virginia. *Mary Cotler: Builder Upon the Red Earth*. Flagstaff, AZ: Northland Press, 1989.

Haich, Elisabeth. *Initiation*. Palo Alto, CA: Seed Center, 1974.

Illich, Ivan. *Gender*. New York: Pantheon, 1982.

Lorenz, Clare. *Women in Architecture: A Contemporary Perspective*. New York: Rizzoli International Publications, 1990.

McQuiston, Liz. *Women in Design: A Contemporary View*. New York: Rizzoli International Publications, 1988.

Showalter, Elaine, editor. *These Modern Women*. New York: The Feminist Press, City University of New York, 1979.

Smith, Jame. *Elsie de Wolfe: A Life in High Style*. New York: Athenaeum, 1982.

Tannen, Deborah. *You Just Don't Understand: Women and Men in Conversation*. New York: Ballantine Books, 1990.

Torre, Susana, editor. *Women in American Architecture: A Historic and Contemporary Perspective*. New York: Whitney Library of Design, 1977.

Wharton, Edith, and Ogden Codman, Jr. *The Decoration of Houses*. New York: W. W. Norton, 1978.

Page numbers in italics refer to illustrations.

A

Ace Architects, 168, *168, 198*
After All (Wharton), 10
Age of Unreason, The (Handy), 31
AIA (American Institute of
    Architects), 14
    awards by, 17, 31, 73, 116,
    127, 175
    women designers and, 10,
    12–13, 117, 166, 175
Allen, Davis, 23, 26, 115, 124,
    160, 175
Allen, Jim, 31
American Institute of Decorators,
    14
Americans with Disabilities Act
    (1992), 11
American Women's Economic
    Development (AWED), 115, 170
Andrea Doria, 16
Architectural Association, 11, 117
Architectural Digest, 125, 169
Architectural League of New York,
    166
architecture:
    academic programs and, 10,
    11, 12, 13, 14, 29; *see also
    individual schools*
    gender divisions in, 10–11,
    13, 73
    interior design vs., 9, 10, 11,
    12, 13, 25, 65, 79, 119, 165
    as male-dominated field, 10,
    11, 12–13, 14, 15, 171
    women designers and, 10–11,
    12, 13, 24–25, 29, 64, 66, 72,
    77, 116, 121, 122, 127, 167,
    168
Architecture, 10
Armstrong, Leslie, 16–17, *16,
    32–35*
    Blanchard Howard Bartlett
    Theater, *33*
    Gay Head house, *32*
    Henry Holt & Company, 17, *17*
    Interiors office, 17, *34*
    Massachusetts house of, 17
    Richards and Hanson house, 16
    Schwartz and Drosd renovation,
    35
    Wilmington Grand Opera, 17
Art for Everyday (Conway), 165
ASID (American Society of Interior
    Designers), 12, 14
    St. Clair and, 74, 75
Astor, John Jacob, 72, 73
"austerity nineties," 126

B

Babey, Pamela, 13, *15*, 160–161,
    160, 176–181
    Doubletree Hotel Plaza,
    180–181
    "In Flight" carpet design, *161*
    "Ratti and Paisley" exhibit
    design, *161*
    Regent Hotel, 161, *176*
    San Francisco law firm, *176*
    Shell headquarters, 161,
    177–179
Babey Moulton, 13, 160
Ball State University, 72, 73
Beal, Louis, 19
Beecher, Catherine, 10
Bellinger, Gretchen, 13, *15*,
    162–163, *162, 182–187*
    0Bellinger offices, 162, *183*
    Camp Bellinger and, 13, *15*,
    162, 186–187
    custom textiles, 162, *162*, 163,
    182, 184–187
    residence of, *182, 184–185*
Bethune, Louisa, 10
Biedermeier furniture, 27
boutique operations, 115
Brennan Beer Gorman
    Monk/Interiors, 72
Bronx Children's Psychiatric
    Facility, 64–65
Buchsbaum, Alan, 17
Burns, Martha, 64, *64–65, 80–83*
    Embassy Suites Hotel, 65, *65,
    82–83*
    Los Angeles Olympics
    Organizing Committee, 65
    Manhattan building renovation,
    81
    National Westminister Bank, 80

C

Cabot Foundation, 64
CAD (computer assisted design),
    11, 20, 21
California, University of, at
    Berkeley, 116, 160, 168
California, University of, at Los
    Angeles, 25
California, University of, at San
    Diego, 13
California Women in
    Environmental Design, 169
Camp Bellinger, 13, *15*, 162,
    186–187
Carmen, Josephine, *see*
    Carmen/Igonda

AWED (American Woman's
    Economic Development),
    115, 170

Carmen/Igonda, 18–19, *18, 36–39*
    Citicorp private facility, *37*
    La Opinion, 38–39
    Leastec Inc., *18*
    North Cherokee offices of, 18, 19
    Sitmar Cruises, *19*
    Stendig showroom, 18
    United Business Interiors, *36*
Carol Groh & Associates, 114
Center for American Design, 113
Chaloner, John, 69
Chicago Interior Design
    Organization, 71
Chicago Merchandise Mart, 30,
    175
Childs, Kirsten, 14
church design, *159*
Cincinnati, University of, 31, 71
client education, 27, 71, 113
Clodagh, 112–13, *112, 128–131*
    American Can Company, 113,
    129
    Bonnie Lunt offices, *129*
    Harrison penthouse, 113, *130*
    Manhattan residence, *131*
    Plush and Sally residence, 113
Clodagh Ross Williams, 113
Codman, Ogden, Jr., 9–10
Colony Club, 9
color, physiology of, 65
Columbia University School of
    Architecture, 13, 16, 21, 164,
    167
Conative Connection, The (Kolbe),
    70
contemporary art, 27, 38
Conway, Patricia, 13, *15*, 124, *124*,
    164–165, *188–193*
    Bally's Park Place Casino Hotel,
    193
    Cleary, Gottlieb, Stearn &
    Hamilton, *191*
    Equitable Life Assurance, 165
    MONY Financial Services, 165,
    191–192
    Nickelodeon, *188*
    private investment offices,
    164, 190
    Viacom, 165, *189*
Cornell University, 21, 118
corporate art collections, 26–27,
    46, 69, 84
corporate facility design, 11, 15
    Eclectics and, 17, 18, 20, 21, 22
    Minimalists and, 118, 120,
    133–135, 140, 144, 147
    Poets and, 161, 177, *177–179,
    211*
    Purists and, 67, 68–69, 73, *85,
    88–90, 94–95*
cost-saving, 21

Cranbrook Academy, 11, 162
Crow, Trammel, 78
custom design:
    Bellinger and, 162, *162*, 163,
    182, 184–187
    carpets, flooring and, 173
    furniture and, 25, 75, *75, 116*,
    117, *117*, 121, *127, 146*, 165
    Helfand and, *116*, 117, *117*
    lighting and, 117, *167*
    Minimalists and, *116*, 117, *117*,
    121, *127, 146*
    Poets and, 161, *161*, 162, *162*,
    163, 165, 167, 182, *184–187*
    textiles and, 65, 161, *161*, 162,
    162, 163, *182, 184–187*

D

Daroff, Karen, 20–21, *20, 40–43*
    Capital Blue Cross, *40*
    Daroff Design Inc., 20, 21
    Levy Gallery, *20*
    Prudential Eastern, 20, 21, *41*
    USG showroom, *41*
    Walt Disney Company, 21,
    42–43
Daroff Design Inc., 20
    Revlon facility, 21
de Armas, Raul, 118, *119*
Decoration of Houses, The
    (Wharton and Codman), 9–10
decorators, 9, 10, 11, 13, 69, 79,
    170
Designer of the Year award, 20,
    23, 115, 164
de Wolfe, Elsie, 9, *9*, 10, 11

E

Eclectics, 15, 32–63
    antiques used by, 23, 24, 27
    corporate facilities design and,
    17, 18, 20, 21, 22
    environmental psychology and,
    28–29, 59
    financial design and, 23, 27, *27,
    36, 37, 54–55*
    historical details and, 18, *32–33*
    hotel design and, 15, *42–43*
    institutional design and, 18, 19,
    20, 28–29, 57, 58–59
    interactive environments and,
    15, 16, 29, 30
    multiple disciplines and, 15, 16,
    18, 21
    office design and, 17, 23, 27, *34,
    38–39, 44–45, 48, 52, 53, 60*
    problem-solving and, 15, 21
    residential design, 16, 17, 24,
    25, 27, *32, 34, 49, 50–51, 63*
    response of, to clients, 15, 19,
    23

retail design and, 23, 31, *61*
showroom design and, 18, 30–31, *41, 61*
taste and, 15, 16, 24
use of color by, 17, 27, *34, 38–39*
use of light by, 19, 29
see also individual designers
environmental awareness, 67
environmental psychology, 28–29, *59*, 67, 112
psychiatric patients and, 64–65
Eva Maddox Associates, 30, 31
Eve's Kinder Garden, 31
exhibit design, 15, *161*
Purists and, 67, *84, 86, 89, 91*

F

facility management, 69, 74
Farnum, John, 18
fast-track designing, 21
feng shui, 113, 114–115
FIDER (Foundation for Interior Design Education Research), 12
Filippi, Dianne, 172
financial design, 11, *80, 190–192*
Eclectics and, 23, 27, *27, 36, 37, 54–55*
Minimalists and, *118, 124*, 125, *125, 154*
Forty Under Forty, 169'
Foster, Norman, 114
Foster-Crowder, Lee, 66–67, *66, 84–87*
C & P Telephone, 67, *85*
Friends of the Earth, 67
Georgetown University, *87*
Hechinger Company, *84*
Kuwait reconstruction project, 66
Public Technology, Incorporated, 67
Smithsonian Ceremonial Court, 67, *67, 86*
U.S. Chamber of Commerce, 67, *86*
Fox, Shelley, 124, 164
Fox & Fowle Architects, 65, 80

G

garden design, *102, 202–203*
gender differences, 10–11, 13–14, 15
Gensler & Associates/Architects, 22, *22*, 23
Georgia State University, 68
Godwin, Gail, 166
Graham, Bruce, 162, 174
Graham, Jane, 14, *14*
Grant, Margo, 22–23, *22, 44–47*, 115

Bank of America, *22*
Covington & Burling, *46*
Cravath, Swaine & Moore, 22, *47*
Gensler & Associates/Architects, 22, *22*, 23, *45*
Newsweek, *45*
Steptoe & Johnson, *44*
Graves, Michael, 22, 121
Gretchen Bellinger Inc., 162, *183*
Groh, Carol, 114–115, *114*, 119, 124, *132–135*
feng shui and, 114–115
J. P. Stevens, *134–135*
Schering-Plough, *133*
Time-Warner, 135
Warner Communications, *114, 132*

H

Halsband, Frances, 13, 166–167, *166, 194–197*
custom lighting, 167
Kliment and Halsband offices, 167
Levine Huntley Schmidt & Beaver, *194*
Marsh & McLennan, *194*
Martha's Vineyard residence, *167*
Princeton University, *166*
Woodstock restaurant, *195*
Woodstock weekend house, *196–197*
Hamilton, Mel, 26
Handy, Charles, 31
Harris, Dorothy, 68–69, *68, 88–91*
Atlanta Committee for the Olympic Games, 68, *88–89*
Atlantic Center Display, *91*
Coca-Cola Enterprises, 68–69, *90*
Rosser Fabrap International, 68, *69*
Royal Saudi Naval Headquarters, 68, *69*
Harvard Business School, 77
Harvard Graduate School of Design, 71, 121, 165
Hawks, Kitty, 24–25, *24, 48–51*
custom furniture by, 25, *48*
Manhattan apartments, *49, 51*
showcase house, *50–51*
talent agency offices, 24, *25, 48*
health-care design, 18, 19, 28, 29
Helfand, Margaret, 116–117, *116, 136–139*
Adlersberg residence, *136*
Buffalo retail store, *137*
Café W furniture, *117*
Cullinane retail store, *136*
Helfand offices, 116, *139*

Jennifer Reed showroom, *138*
Table in Six Segments, *116*
hospice design, 29, *58–59*
hospital design, 12, 19, *57, 64–65*
hospitality design, 18, 75, 76–77, 79
see also hotel design; restaurant design
hotel design, 11, 15
Eclectics and, 15, *42–43*
Poets and, 161, 162, 163, *176, 180–181, 193, 210, 212–213*
Purists and, 15, 65, 72, 73, 74, 75, 76–77, 78, *82–83, 96–102, 103, 105, 107, 108–109, 110–111*
hotel renovations, 72, *96–99*
House in Good Taste, The (Wharton), 10
Howard, Lucia, 168–169, *168, 198–203*
Ace Architects, 168
Berkeley residence, *201*
Community Travel Service, *201*
Country Store, 168
Lakeside Delicatessen, 168–169, *202–203*
Montclair residence, *200*
"Psycho-Remodel," *198–199*
San Francisco residence, *200*

I

IBD (Institute of Business Designers), 18, 67, 124
IFMA (International Facilities Management Association), 69
Igonda, Clara, *see* Carmen/Igonda
IIDC (Illinois Interior Design Coalition), 71
Illinois, University of, 31
Illinois Institute of Technology, 11
image making, 26, 27
I. M. Pei & Partners, 120, 121; *see also* Pei Cobb Freed & Partners
Innerplan, 124, 152
Inside Out Design, 21
institutional design:
Eclectics and, 18, 19, *20*, 28–29, *57, 58–59*
hospices, 29, *58–59*
hospitals, 12, 19, *57, 64–65*
Minimalists and, 121, 123, *144, 145, 146, 159*
Poets and, *166*, 172, *172*, 173, *206–207*
Purists and, 64–65, *68, 69, 87*
see also exhibit design
interior architecture, 23, 31
interior design, commercial:
architecture vs., 9, 10, 11, 12, 13, 25, 65, 79, 119, 165

companies run by women in, 9, 10–11, 14, 21, 26, 66–67, 68
decorators and, 9, 10, 11, 13
de Wolfe and, 9, 10, 11
economic indicators and, 11–12, 127
future consolidation of, 14–15
gender divisions and, 10–11, 13, 14, 16, 165, 169
history and development of, 9–15
legislation and, 11, 12, 165
marketing and, 18–19, 20, 25, 30–31, 79, 115, 163, 172
narrative ideas and, 13–14
recognition of women in, 12–13
residential design vs., 10, 11, 17, 24, 25, 27, 74
women's movement and, 12, 14, 15, 16
see also individual designers and fields
interior design, residential, *see* residential design
Interior Design Hall of Fame, 23, 75, 127, 175
Interiors, 17, 29, 34, 120
Designer of the Year award and, 20, 23, 115, 164
International Style, 11
Isozaki, Arata, 22, 24
Iu, Carolyn, 118–119, *118, 140–143*
Chase Manhattan Bank, *118*
Citicorp offices, *141*
Haj Terminal, 119
Manufacturers Hanover, *143*
Merrill Lynch, 118, 119, *140*
One Liberty Plaza, *142*
Palio desk accessories, *119*

J

John Carl Warnecke Associates, 124, 164, 171
Johnson, Philip, 23, 169
joint ventures, 19, 29, 66, 125, 172

K

Kahn, Louis I., 167
Kallmann McKinnell & Wood, 120, 121
Keating, Rick, 26
Kentucky, University of, 26
Kenyon, Paul, 19
Kleinschmidt, Robert, 115, 163, 174
Kliment, Robert, 167, *194*
Kling, Vincent, 20
Knoll, Florence Schust, 11, *11*, 124
Knoll Group, 11, 69, 75, 119, 127, 161, 163
Knoll Planning Unit, 11, 124

Kohn, Eugene, 124, 164
Kolbe, Kathy, 70, 71
Kolbe Concept, 70
KPFC (Kohn Pedersen Fox
    Conway), 164–165, *189,*
    191–192

L

large-scale projects, 21, 174, 175
Larsen, Jack Lenor, 65
Larson, George, 163, 174
leadership styles, 13–14, 166
lease negotiation, 74
Lee, Sarah Tomerlin, 14, *14*
Leff, Naomi, 170–171, *170,*
    204–209
    Arcade at Citicorp, *208–209*
    Beaver Creek Conference
        Center, *206–207*
    Bloomingdale's, 171
    Gulfstream IV, *170*
    Holt Renfrew, *170*
    Polo/Ralph Lauren, 170, 171,
        204–205
Legge, Diane (Diane Legge Kemp),
    14, *14,* 174
Lehman-Smith, Debra, 26–27,
    52–55
    Baker & Botts, *53*
    corporate art collections, 26–27
    Ross Dixon & Masback, 27
    Sun Bank, 26, 27, *27, 54*
    Texas Commerce Bank, *54–55*
    U.S. Olympic Committee, 26, 27
    Vinson & Elkins, *52*
Lehman-Smith Wiseman, 26
Little House, The (Armstrong), 17
Love, Dian, 28–29, *28, 56–59*
    Atlantic City Convention Center,
        56
    Detroit Receiving Hospital, 29,
        57
    Duke University, 28
    Easler House, 29, *58–59*
    Walden Pond residence, 28
Lynford, Ruth, 12, *12*

M

McClintock, Elizabeth, 122–123,
    122, 148–151
    America restaurant, 122, 123,
        149
    Café Greco, *150*
    Ernie's restaurant, 123
    Flatiron restaurant, *149*
    Liberty Café, *151*
    Promostyl showroom, 123
    Union Station restaurant, *148*
McConnell, Patrick, 163, 174
McCurry, Margaret, 174–175, *174,*
    214–217

American Standard, 175, *216*
Chicago Bar Association, 174,
    174, 175, *217*
custom designs, 175, *175*
Herman Miller showroom, 175
Interiors, 175
SOM and, 115, 163, 174–175
Wit's End, *214–215*
Maddox, Eva, 30–31, *30, 60–63*
    AGI showroom, 30–31, *30*
    Collins & Aikman, *62*
    Cynthia retail store, *61*
    Du Pont showroom, *61*
    Hawthorne Realty, *60*
    Maddox residence, *63*
    University of Illinois, *62*
Mallis, Stephanie, 120–121, *120,*
    144–147
    Becton Dickinson, 120, 121, *144*
    Groton School, 121, *146*
    Harvard Business School, 121,
        145
    Hynes Convention Center, 120,
        120, 121, *144*
Mandolfo, Anthony, 124–125
Mangurian, Robert, 25
Marin County Civic Center, 169
Martin-Vegue, Phyllis, 13, *15,*
    172–173, 172, 210–213
    Apple Computer, *211*
    Cheeca Lodge, *173, 213*
    Highlands Inn, *212*
    Hotel Le Meridien, 173, *210*
    Main Library of San Francisco,
        172
    Stanford University, *172, 173*
    Massachusetts Institute of
        Technology (MIT), 127
Maxman, Susan, *12,* 13
medical-research design, 28–29
Megatrends (Naisbitt), 162
Meier, Richard, 65, 121
Mekus, Spes, 70–71, *70, 92–95*
Mekus-Johnson Inc., 70
    Coopers & Lybrand, *70,* 71
    Masuda, Funai, Eifert &
        Mitchell, *94–95*
    Mekus-Johnson Inc., 70, *71*
    Santa Fe Southern Pacific
        Corporation, *92*
    SPSS Inc., *93*
MGS Architects, 122, 123
Miami, University of, 76, 77
Michigan, University of, 29, 173
Miller, Herman, 11, 23, 75
Minimalists, 15, 112–156
    corporate facility design and,
        118, 120, *133–135, 140, 144,*
        147
    custom design and, *116,* 117,
        117, 121, *127, 146*

financial design and, 15, *118,*
    124, 125, *125, 154*
institutional design and, 121,
    123, *144, 145, 146, 159*
neutral backgrounds and, 15,
    112, 115
office design and, 15, 113, *114,*
    128–129, 141, 143, 157
residential design and, 113, 125,
    130–131, 136, 152–153
restaurant design and, 15, 112,
    123, *145, 148–151*
retail design and, 15, 113, 125,
    136–137, 154–155
showroom design and, 15, 123,
    138, 156–157
simplicity and, 112, 113, 115,
    117
see also individual designers
Modernist style, 11, 15, 19, 25, 112
Monk, Julia, 72–73, *72, 96–99*
    corporate offices, *72*
    Gallery Urban, *73*
    Juffali Headquarters, *73*
    St. Regis Hotel, 72, 73, *96–99*
Moore, Charles, 25, 64
Moore College of Art, 20
Morgan, Julia, *9,* 10
Moris, Lamberto, 172

N

Naisbitt, John, 162
National Association of Women
    in Business, 115
National Council of Architectural
    Registration, 119
National Council of Interior
    Design, 175
Neocon, 30, 175
North Carolina State University,
    66, 67

O

office design:
    Eclectics and, 17, 23, 27, *34,*
        38–39, 44–45, 48, 52, 53, 60
    Minimalists and, 113, *114,*
        128–129, 141, 143, 157
    Poets and, 162, *168,* 175, *176,*
        183, 188–189, 191, 194
    Purists and, 67, 74, *103*
one-stop shopping, 26
Oregon, University of, 23
Ornamentalism (Conway), 165
"outdoors indoors," 175
Owen, Sylvia, 124–125, *124,*
    152–155
    Charles Jourdan store, 125, *155*
    Commerzbank, 125, *125, 154*
    Davidoff store, *154*
    residence of, 125, *152*

Texas residence, *153*
Trump Tower stores, 125, *155*
Owen & Mandolfo, 124, 125

P

Parish, Sister, 14, 25
Parsons School of Design, 13, 75,
    115, 171
participatory management, 23
Payette Associates, 28, 29, 120
Pedersen, William, 124, 164
Pei, I. M., 24, 25, 48, 53, 114, 120
Pei Cobb Freed & Partners, 121,
    172
Pennsylvania, University of, 13,
    164, 167
performing arts design, 17, *33*
Perkins & Will, 66, 72–73
Pfister, Charles, 23, 115, 160, 161
Poets, 15, 160–217
    corporate facilities and, 161,
        177, *177–179, 211*
    custom design and, 161, *161,*
        162, 162, 163, 165, 167, *182,*
        184–187
    detail and, 15, 161, 167
    financial design and, *190–192*
    hotel design and, 161, 162, 163,
        176, 180–181, 193, 210,
        212–213
    institutional design, *166,* 172,
        172, 173, 206–207
    large-scale projects and, 174,
        175
    office design and, 162, *168,*
        175, *176, 183, 188–189, 191,*
        194
    residential design and, *167, 182,*
        184–185, 196–197, 198–201,
        214–215
    retail design and, 168, 170, *170,*
        171, *201, 204–205, 208–209*
    showroom design and, 175, *216*
    texture, color, crafting and, 15,
        160, 165
    see also individual designers
Postmodernist style, 11, 15, 125,
    126, 165
Powell, Donald, 115, 163, 174
Pratt Institute, 13, 120, 122, 166,
    170, 171
predesign phase, 21, 164–165
Predock, Antoine, 77, 78
pro bono services, 17, 67, 171
Pulgram, William, 68
Purdue University, 29
Purists, 15, 64–108
    antique details and, 15, 64,
        77, *108*
    client's personality and, 70–71,
        77

corporate facility design and, 67, 68–69, 73, *85, 88–90, 94–95*
environmental psychology and, 64–65, 67
exhibit design and, 67, *84, 86, 89,* 91
historical styles and, 15, 64, 72, 75, 77, *104–106, 108*
hotel design and, 15, 65, 72, 73, 74, 75, 76–77, 78, *82–83, 96–102, 103, 105, 107, 108–109, 110–111*
institutional design and, 64–65, 68, 69
large-scale projects and, 66–67, 68–69, 73–74
office design and, 67, 74, *103*
residential design and 74, *104*
restaurant design and, 15, 74, 75, 76–77, 78–79, *102*
use of color by, 65, 66, 67, 75, *82, 84, 86*
use of light by, 65, 71, 75
see also individual designers
Putman, Andrée, 24, 25

Q

Quick Starts, 70, 71

R

Rainey, J. Woodson, Jr., *189, 191*
Rappoport, James, 21
remodeling, 11–12
residential design, 10, 11
Eclectics and, 16, 17, 24, 25, 27, *32, 34, 49, 50–51, 63*
Minimalists and, 113, 125, *130–131, 136, 152–153*
Poets and, *167, 182, 184–185, 196–197, 198–201, 214–215*
Purists and, 74, *104*
restaurant design, 18, *193*
Minimalists and, 112, 123, *145, 148–151*
Purists and, 15, 74, 75, 76–77, 78–79, *102*
"restyled classic" fabrics, 163
retail design, 11, 15, *81*
Eclectics and, 23, 31, *61*
Minimalists and, 113, 125, *136–137, 154–155*
Poets and, 168, 170, *170, 171, 201, 204–205, 208–209*
Rhode Island School of Design, 29
"Room at the Top" (Scott Brown), 10
Rossbach, Sarah, 114

S

St. Clair, Rita, 74–75, *74, 100–103*

ASID and, 74, 75
custom chairs, *75*
Hotel Intercontinental, 75, 102
Inn at the Colonnade, 75, 103
Netherland Plaza Hotel, 75, *100–101*
private residence, *74*
U.S. Fidelity and Guaranty, 103
San Francisco Organization of Women Architects, 169
Santos, Adele, 13
Scott Brown, Denise, 10, *10*
showroom design, 15, 67, 175, *216*
Eclectics and, 18, 30–31, *41, 61*
Minimalists and, 123, *138, 156–157*
Simon, Cathy, 172
Simon Martin-Vegue Winkelstein Moris, 172–173
Skidmore Owings & Merrill (SOM), 36, *71,* 120, 123, 127
Allen and, 23, 26, 115, 119, 124, 160, 175
Babey and, 160–161
Bellinger and, 162–163
Iu and, 118, 119
Legge Kemp and, 14, 174
Lehman-Smith and, 26, 27
McCurry and, 115, 163, 174–175
Space for Dance (Armstrong), 17
space planning, 23, 67, 74
sports facility design, 27, 65, 76, *106, 110*
Stendig International, 18, 25, 127
Stern, Robert A.M., 78, 169
Sweet's catalogs, 11

T

Texas, University of, at Austin, 78, 79
theater design, 17, *33,* 75
Thompson, Jane, 14, *14*
Tigerman, Stanley, 31, 174, 175
Tigerman McCurry, 174, *217*
Torre, Susana, 13, *15,* 171
"traditional" style, 19, 25
Trisha Wilson & Associates, 78, 79, 108

U

Ueberroth, Peter, 65
unified concept, 76–77

V

value-added services, 23
Vignelli, Lella, 126–127, *126, 156–159*
Artemide showroom, *157*
Poltrona Frau showrooms, *156, 158*

St. Peter's Church, *127, 159*
Saratoga furniture line, *127*
Vignelli Associates offices, 126, *157*
Vignelli, Massimo, 126, 127
Vignelli Associates, 126, *157*
Vision 2000, 12

W

Warnecke, John Carl "Jack," 124–125
Weingarten, David, 168
Wharton, Edith, 9–10, *9*
Willis, Beverly, 10, *10*
Wilson, Lynn, 76–78, *76,* 104–107
Biltmore Hotel restoration, 76, 77, *104*
Boca Raton Hotel and Beach Club, *106*
Coral Gables Golf Club, *105*
residence of, 77, *104*
Rittenhouse Hotel, 77, *77*
Wilson, Trisha, 78–79, *78,* 108–111
Anatole Hotel, 78–79
Four Seasons Hotel and Resort, *108*
Horizon Condominium, *109*
Hotel Bel-Air Cap-Ferrat, *108*
Inn of the Anasazi, *111–112*
Palace Hotel, 79
St. Andrew's Old Course Hotel, *110*
Waterfront Centre Hotel, *78*
Winkelstein, Peter, 172
women designers:
academia and, 10, 11, 13, 14, 29, 31, 164, 165
AIA and, 10, 12–13, 117, 166, 175
architecture training and, 10–11, 12, 13, 24–25, 29, 64, 66, 72, 77, 116, 121, 122, 127, 167, 168
awards to, 26, 30, 75, 116, 120, 124, 125, 126; *see also individual awards*
companies set up by, 9, 10–11, 14, 18, 21, 26, 66–67, 68, 76, 77, 78, 115, 163, 169, 170, 171, 175
male architects vs. 10, 13, 16, 65, 165
training of, 10, 11, 13, 14, 75, 119; *see also individual schools see also individual designers and fields*
Workbook Approach, 21
Working Woman, 17, 34
Wright, Frank Lloyd, 11, 62, 71, 169

Y

Yale School of Architecture, 64, 122, 123
Young President's Organization, 77, 79